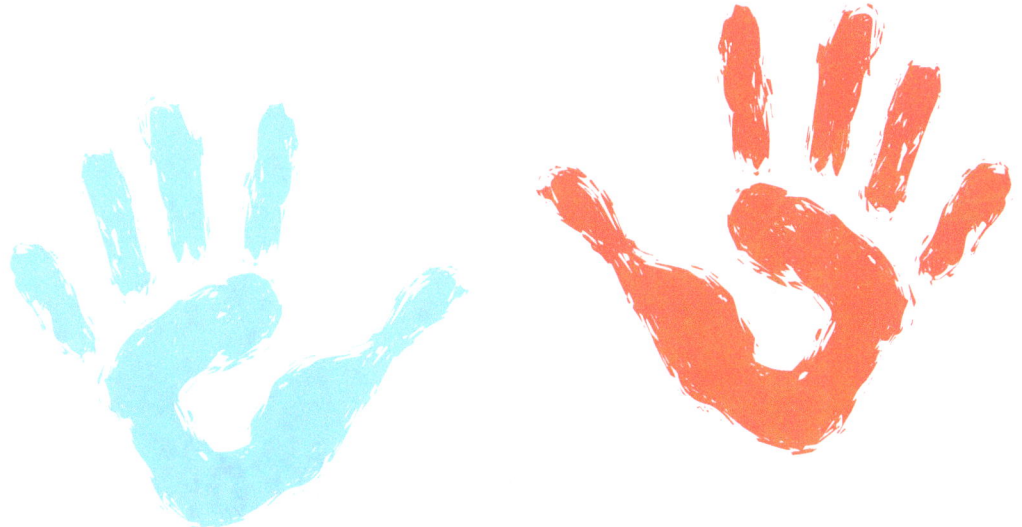

I am grateful to God for everything! And I believe that the meaning of life is to give meaning to other lives.

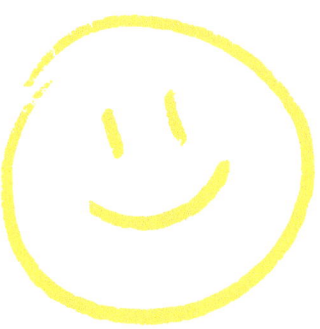

Welisson Silva

2024

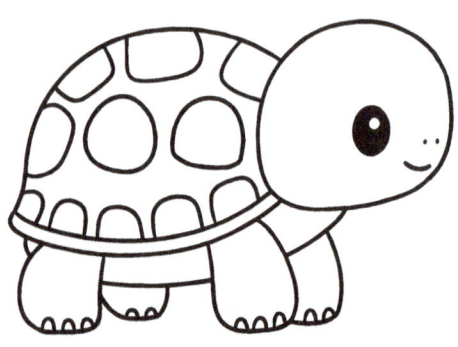
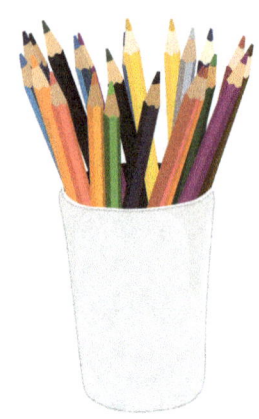

# This Book Belongs to:

_____

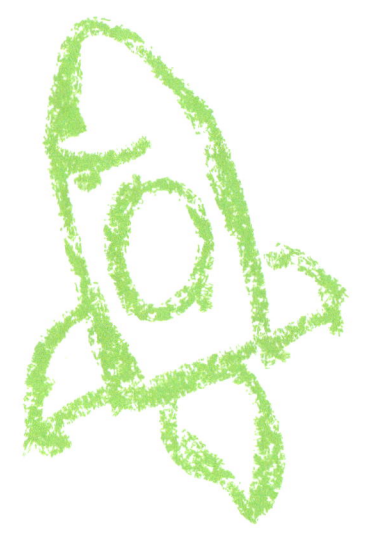
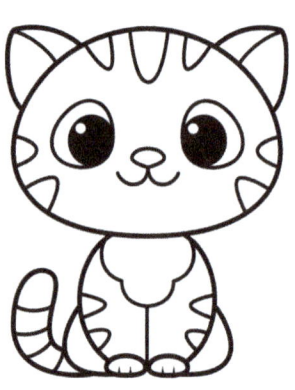

w.s.p. ©
all rights reserved

# ALL RIGHTS RESERVED©
# 2024

**No part of this publication may be reproduced, distributed, or transmitted in any form or by any means, including photocopying, recording, or other electronic or mechanical methods, without the prior written permission of the publisher, except for brief quotations incorporated in critical reviews and other specific noncommercial uses. Any unauthorized replica of this work is prohibited.**

**W.S.P.©**

# Test Color Page

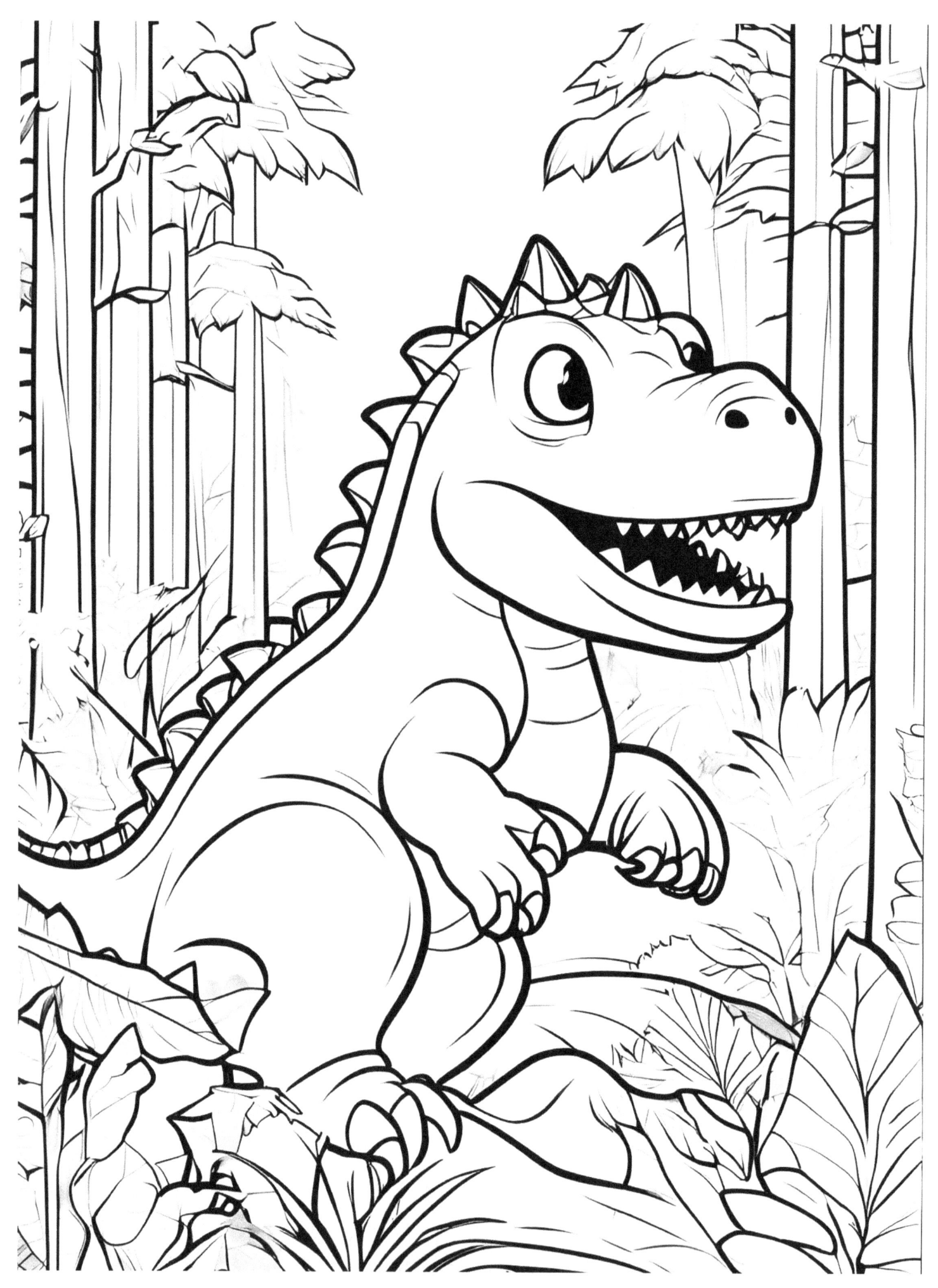

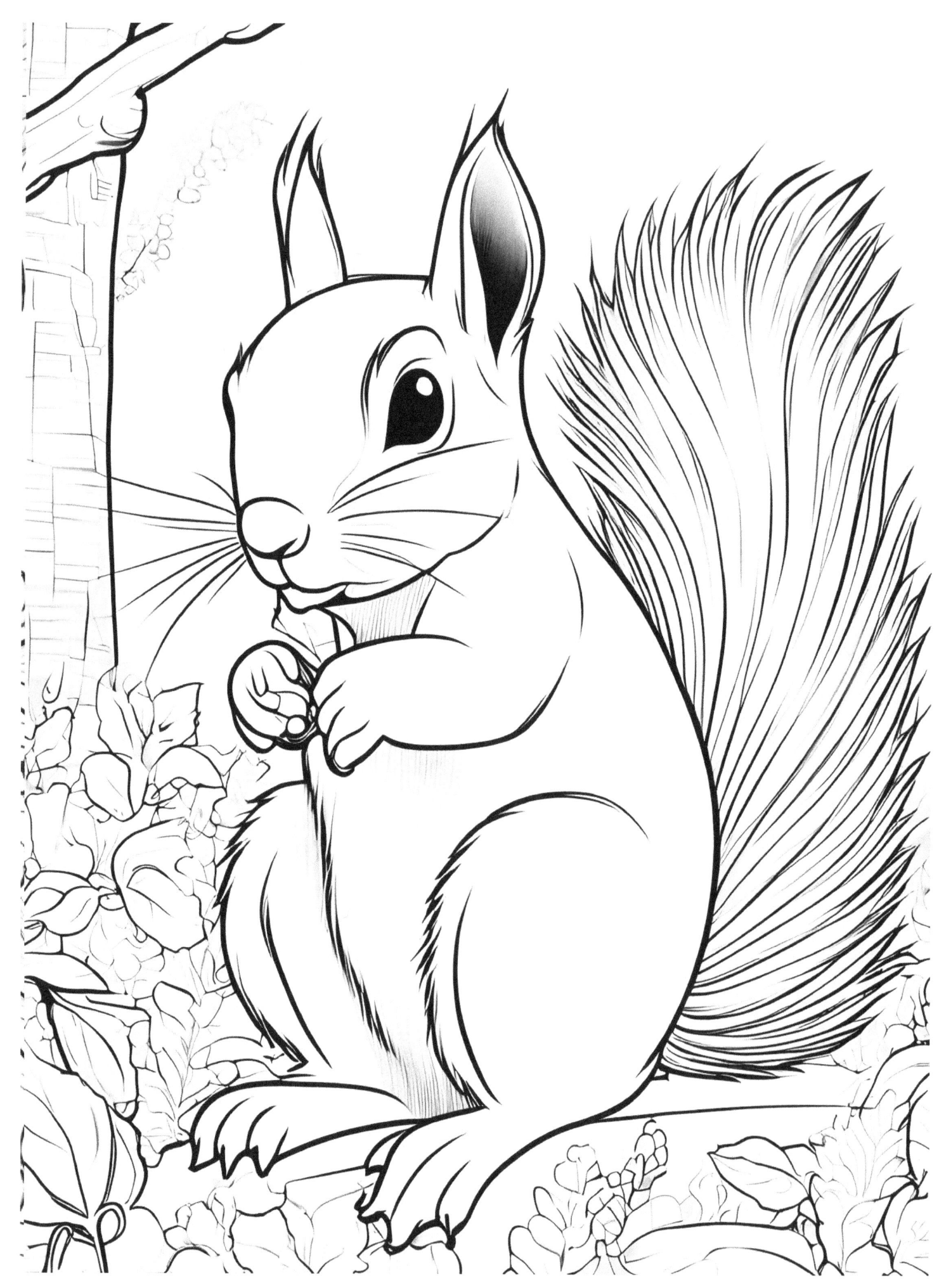

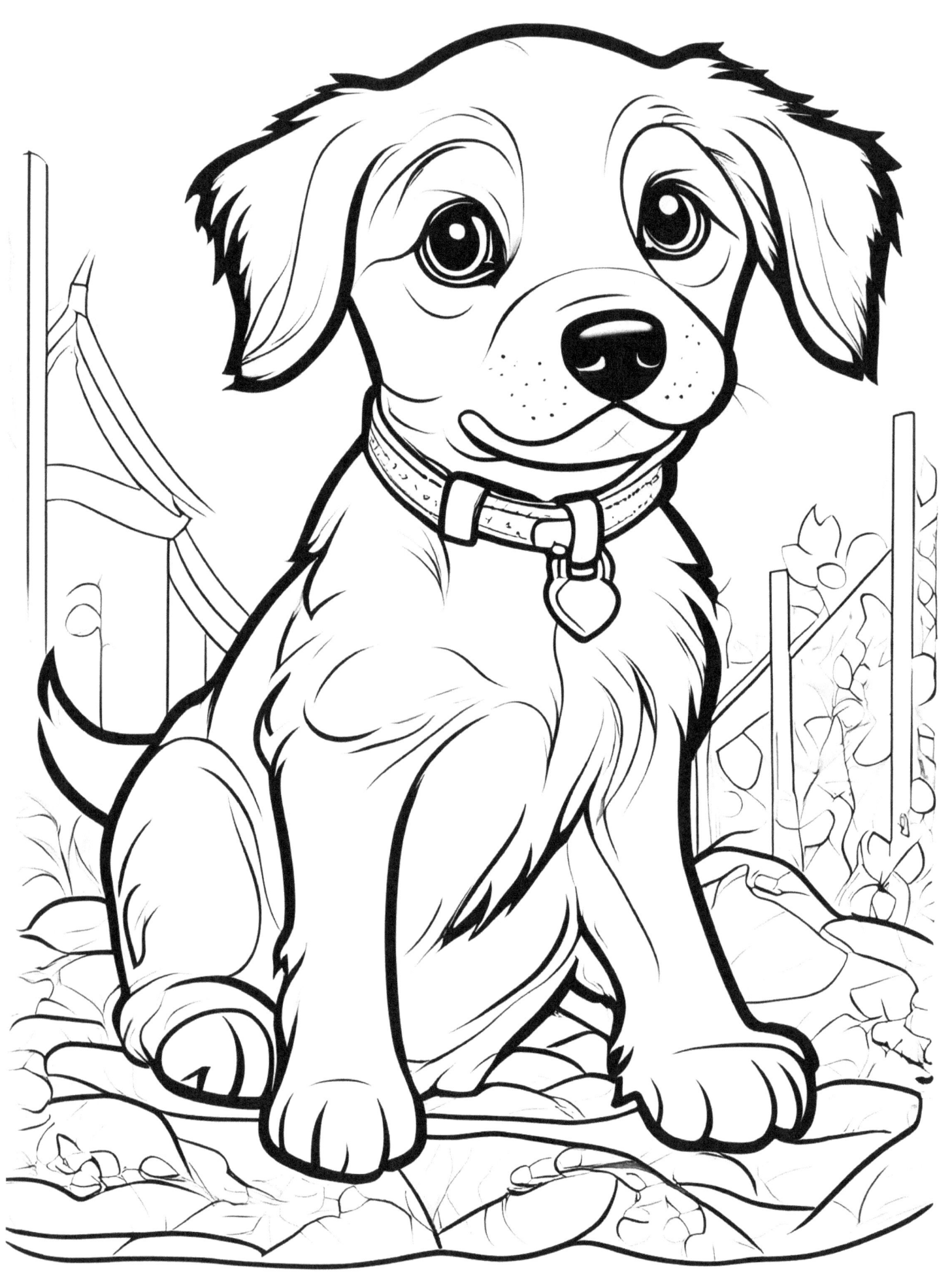

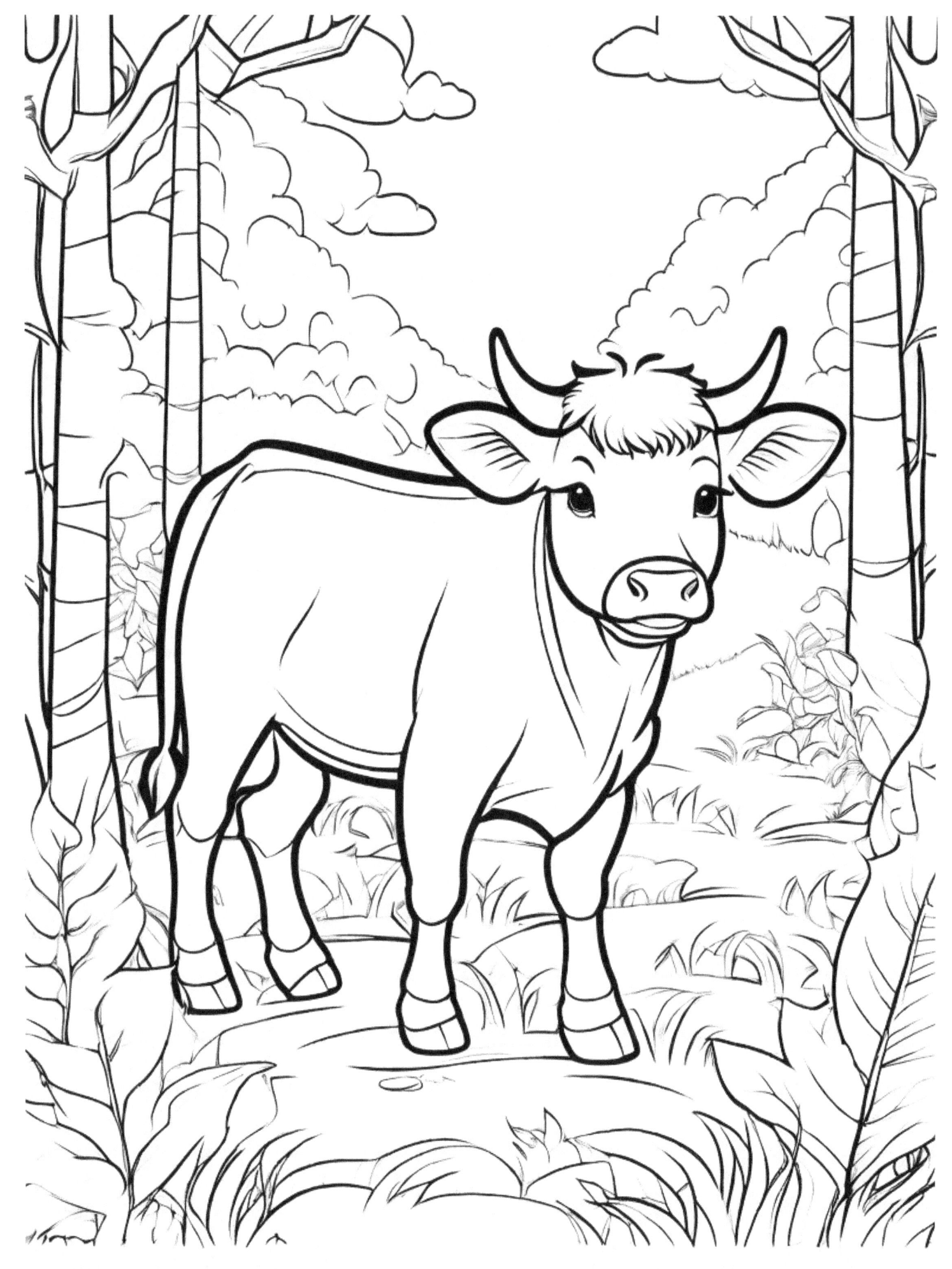

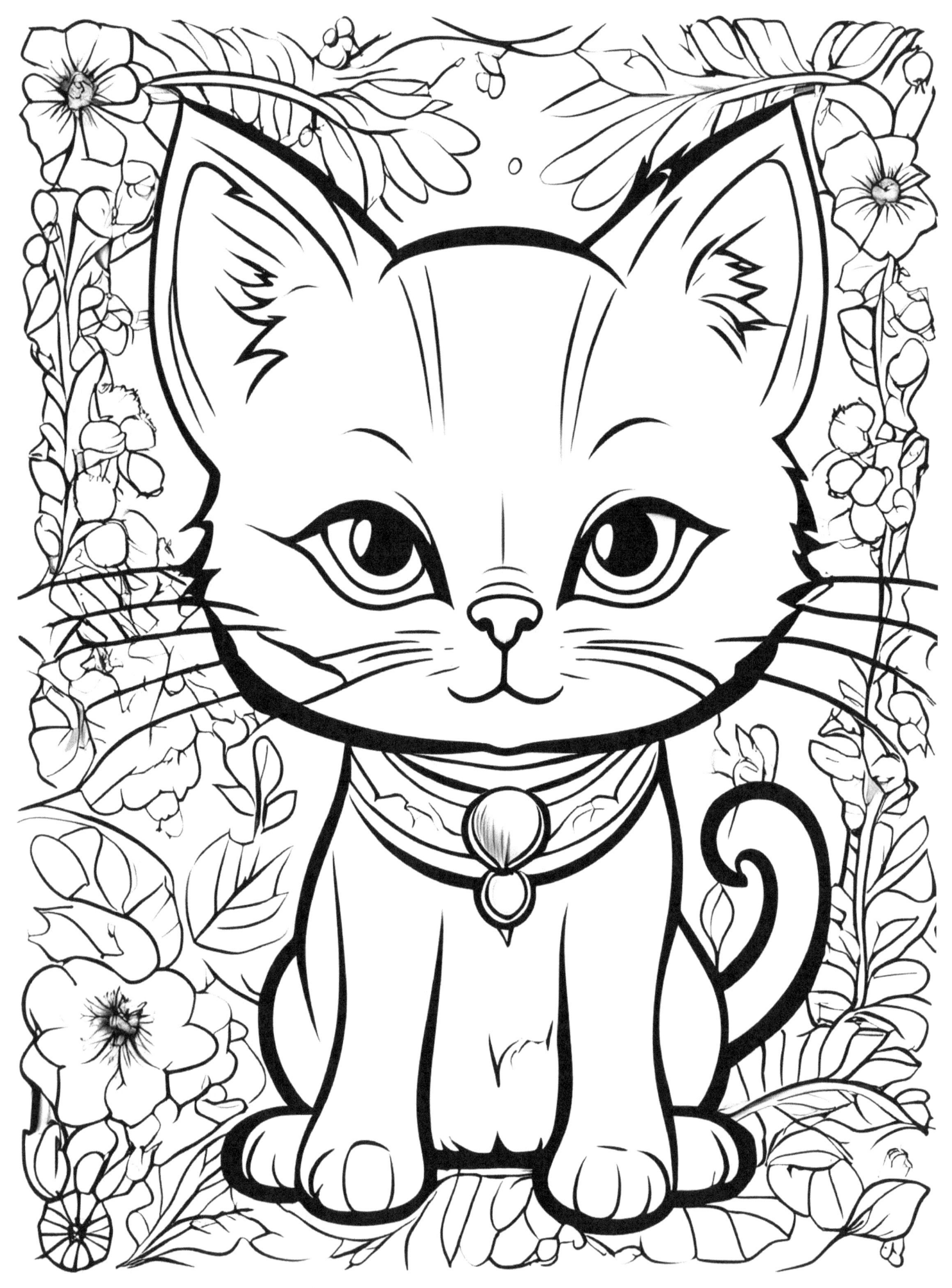

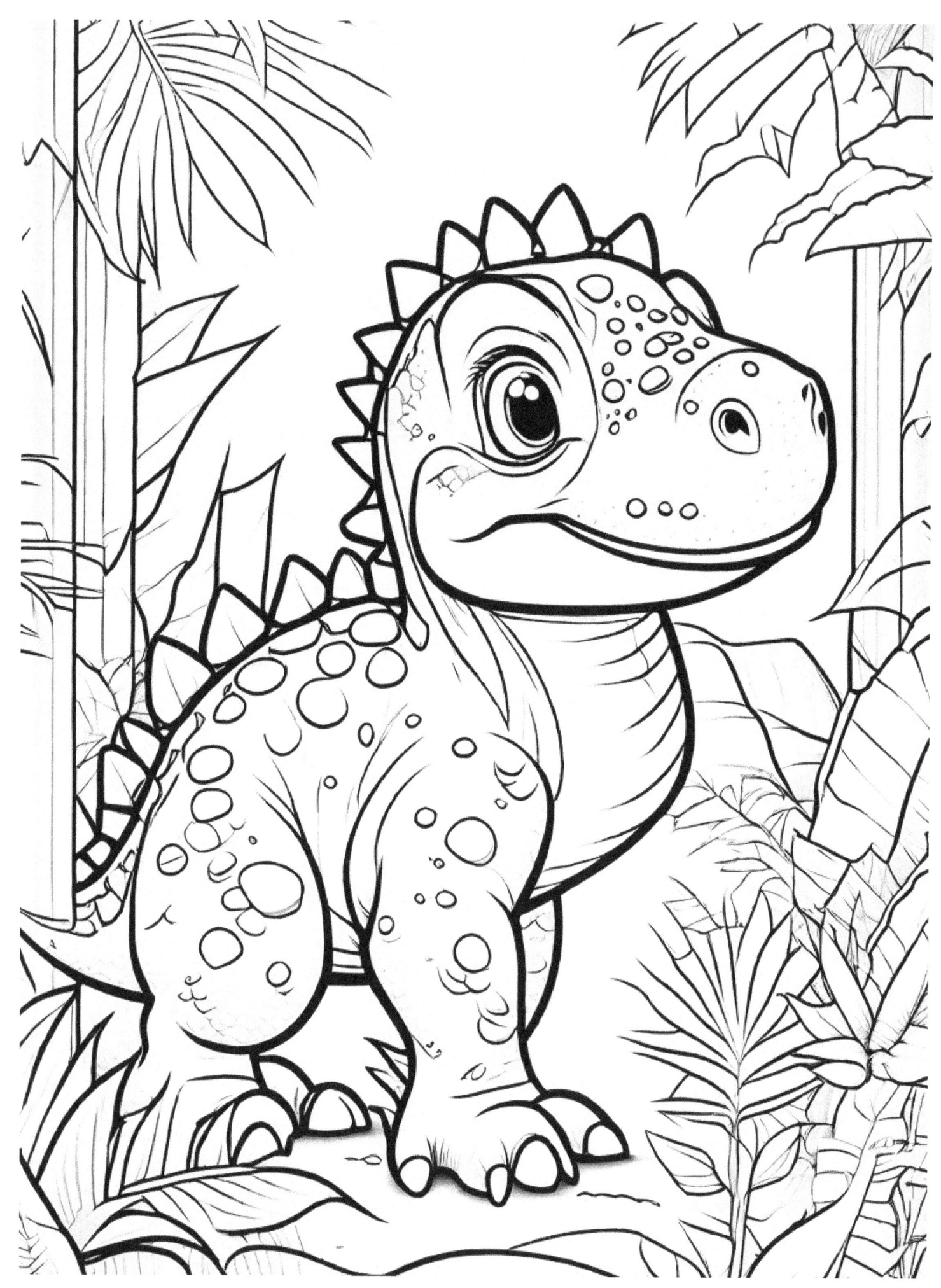

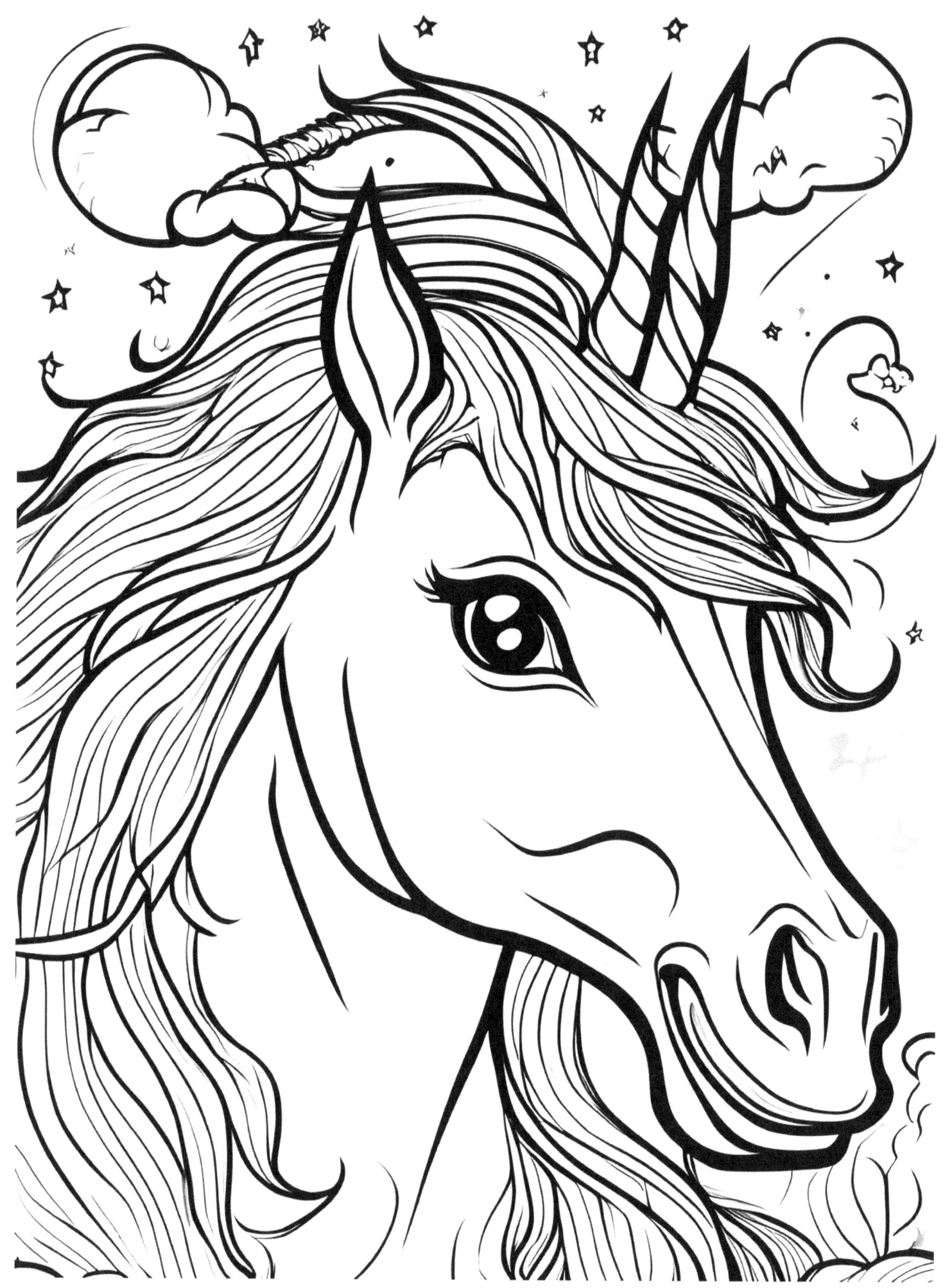

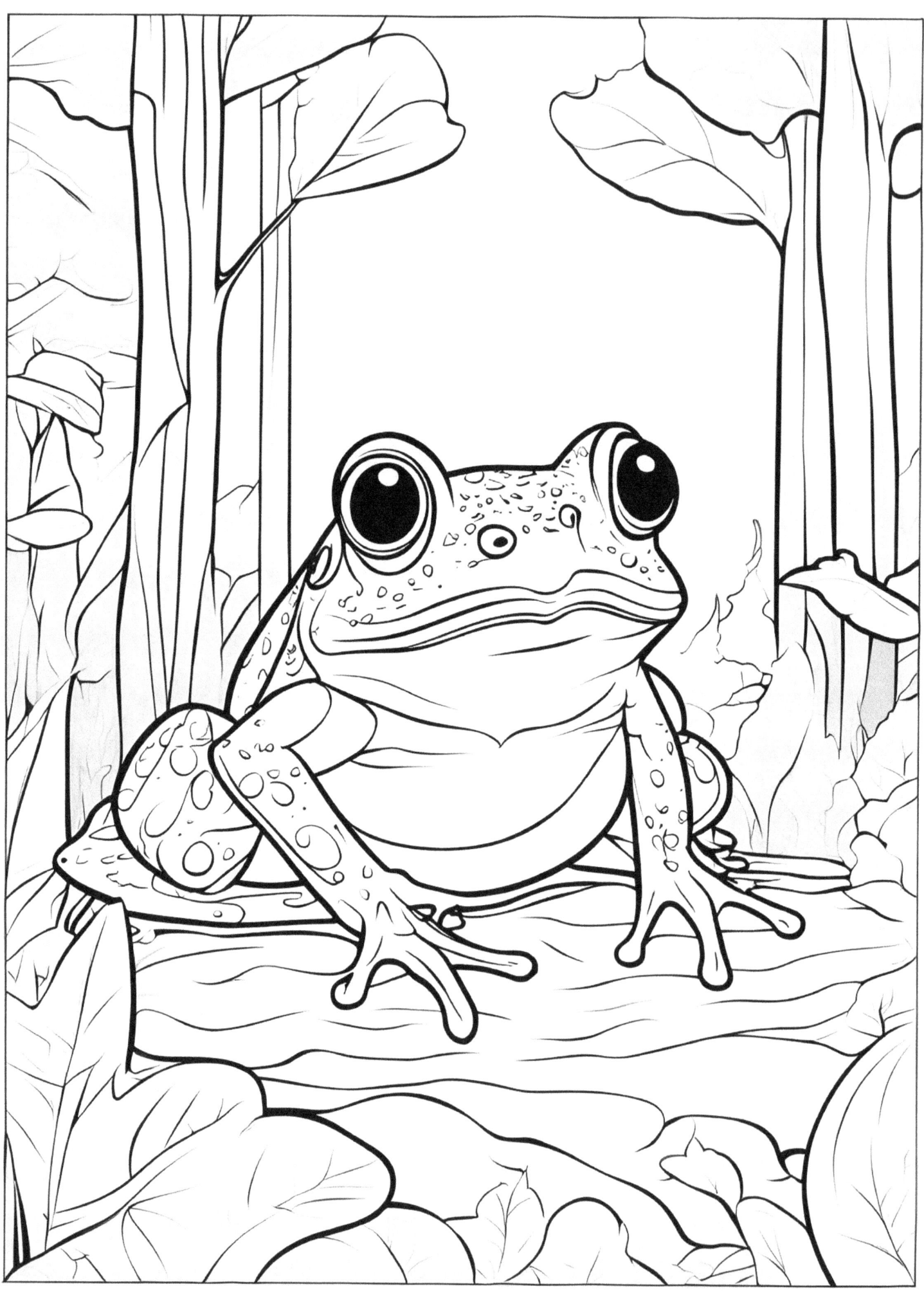

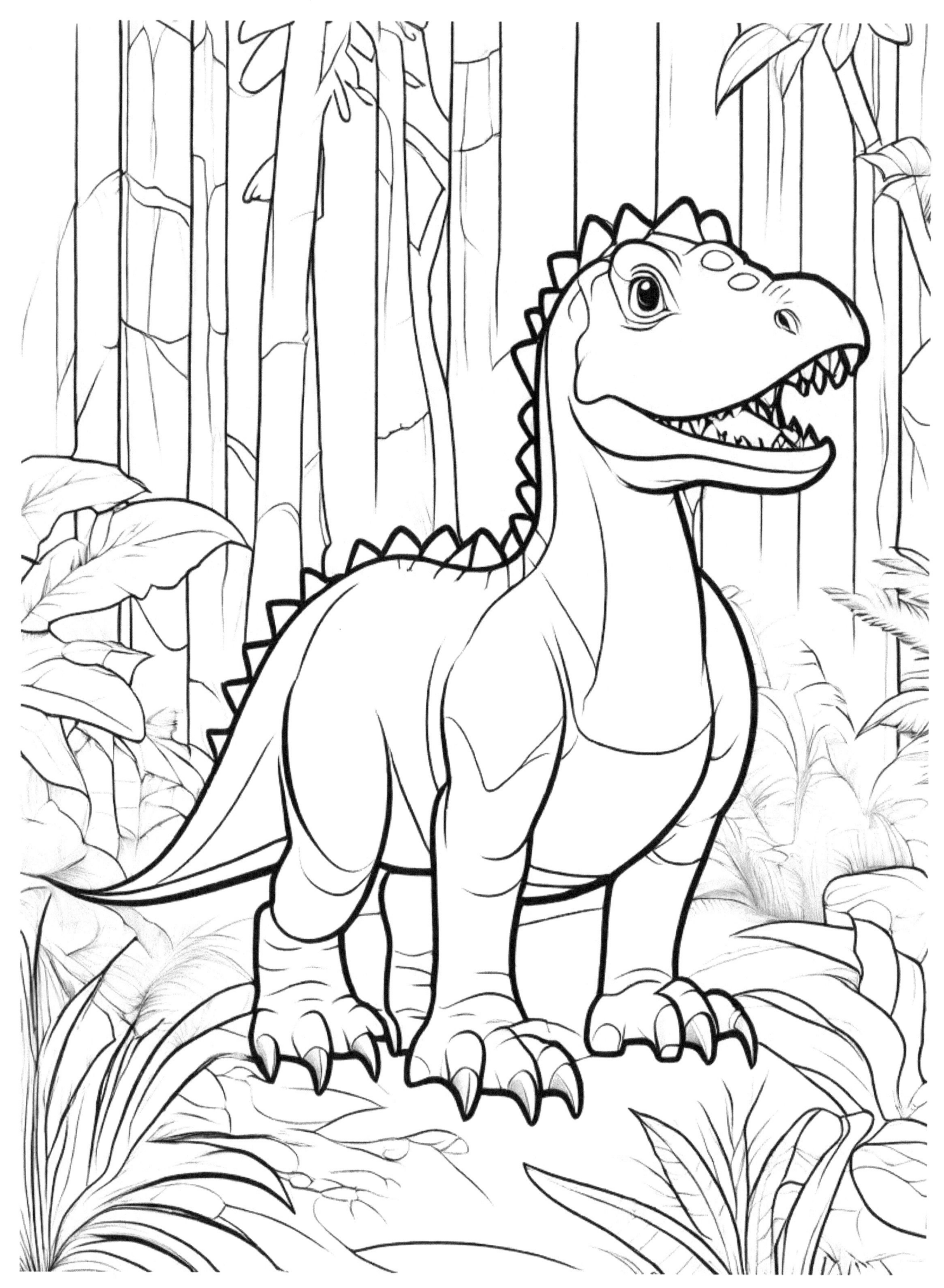

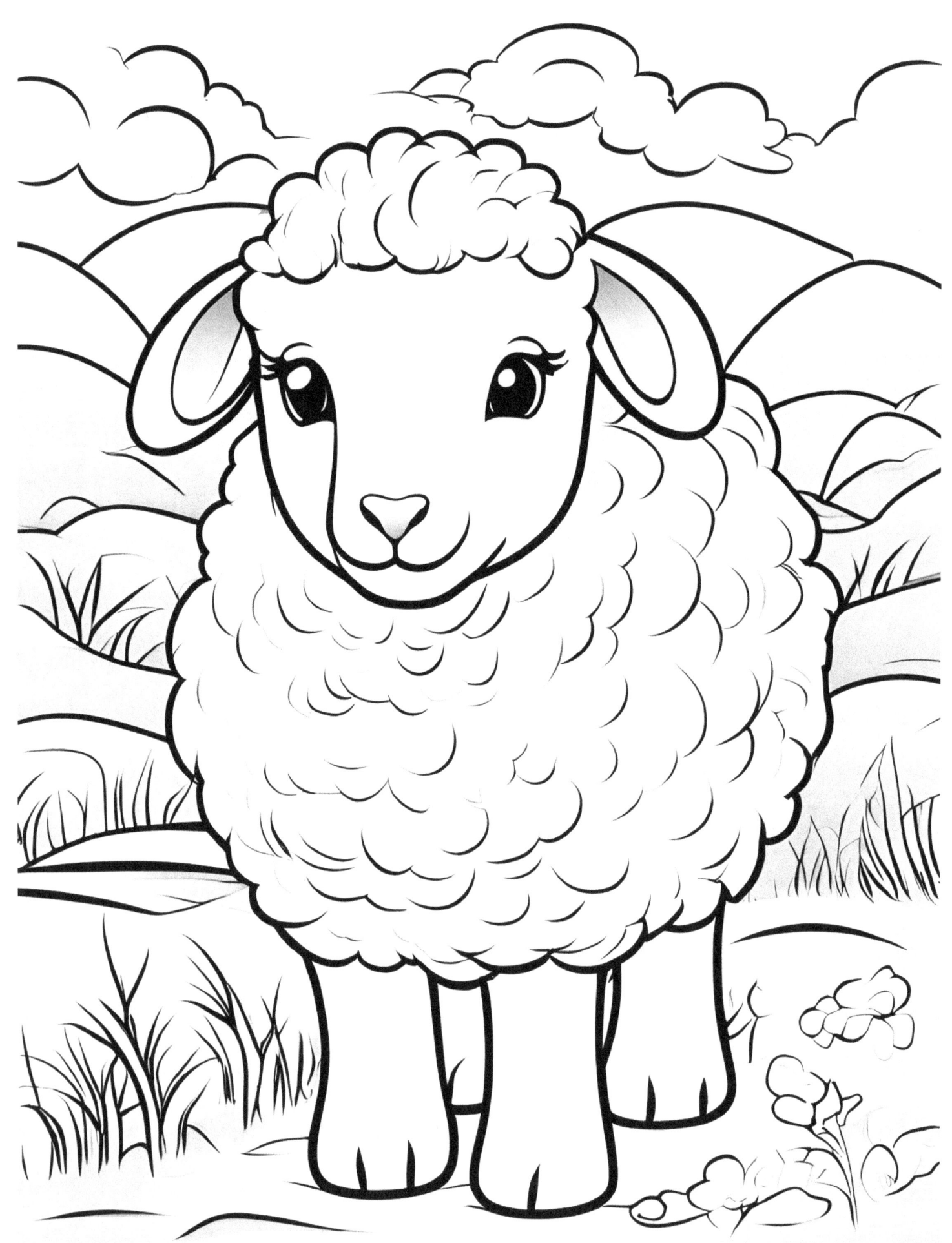

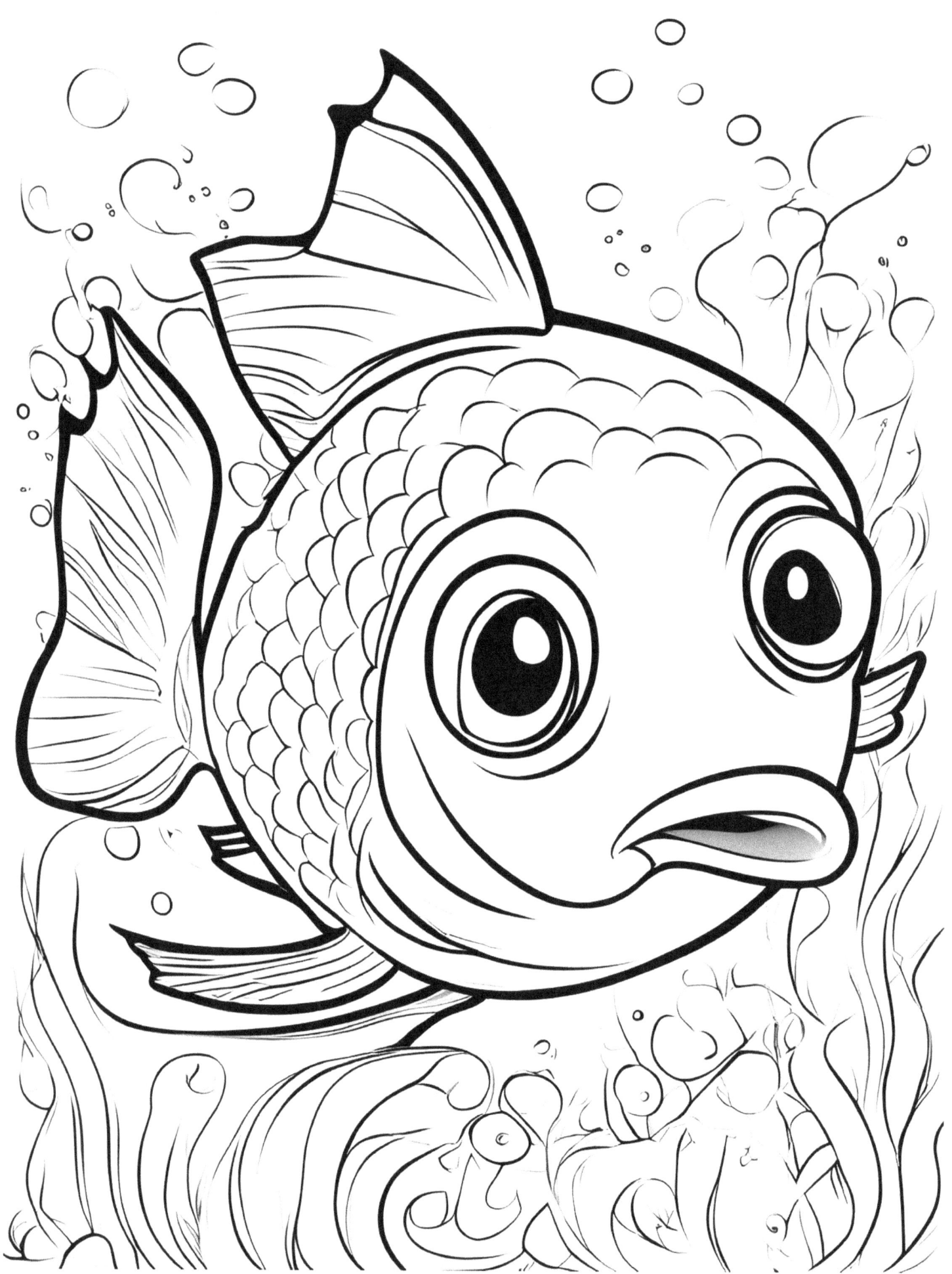

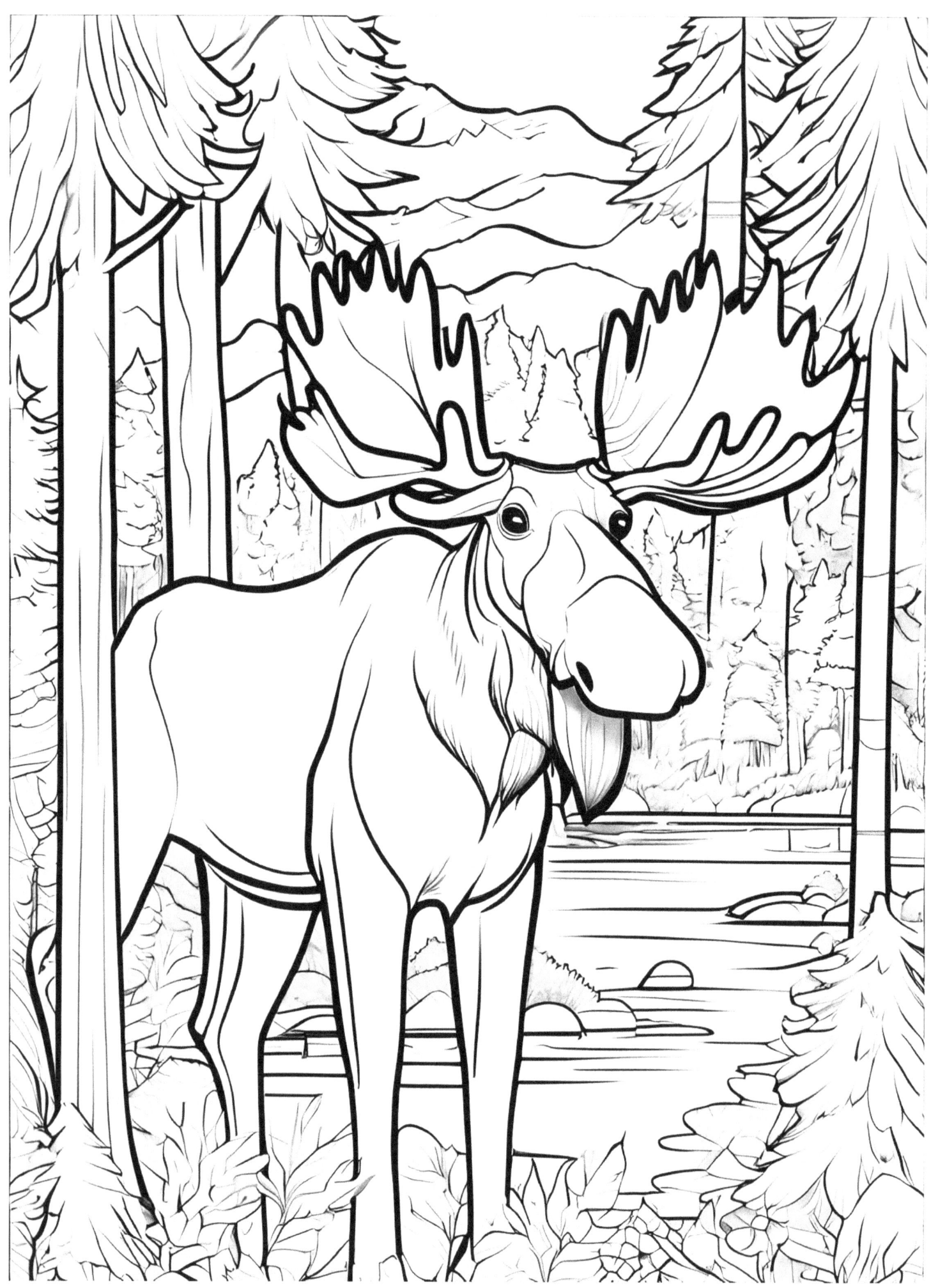

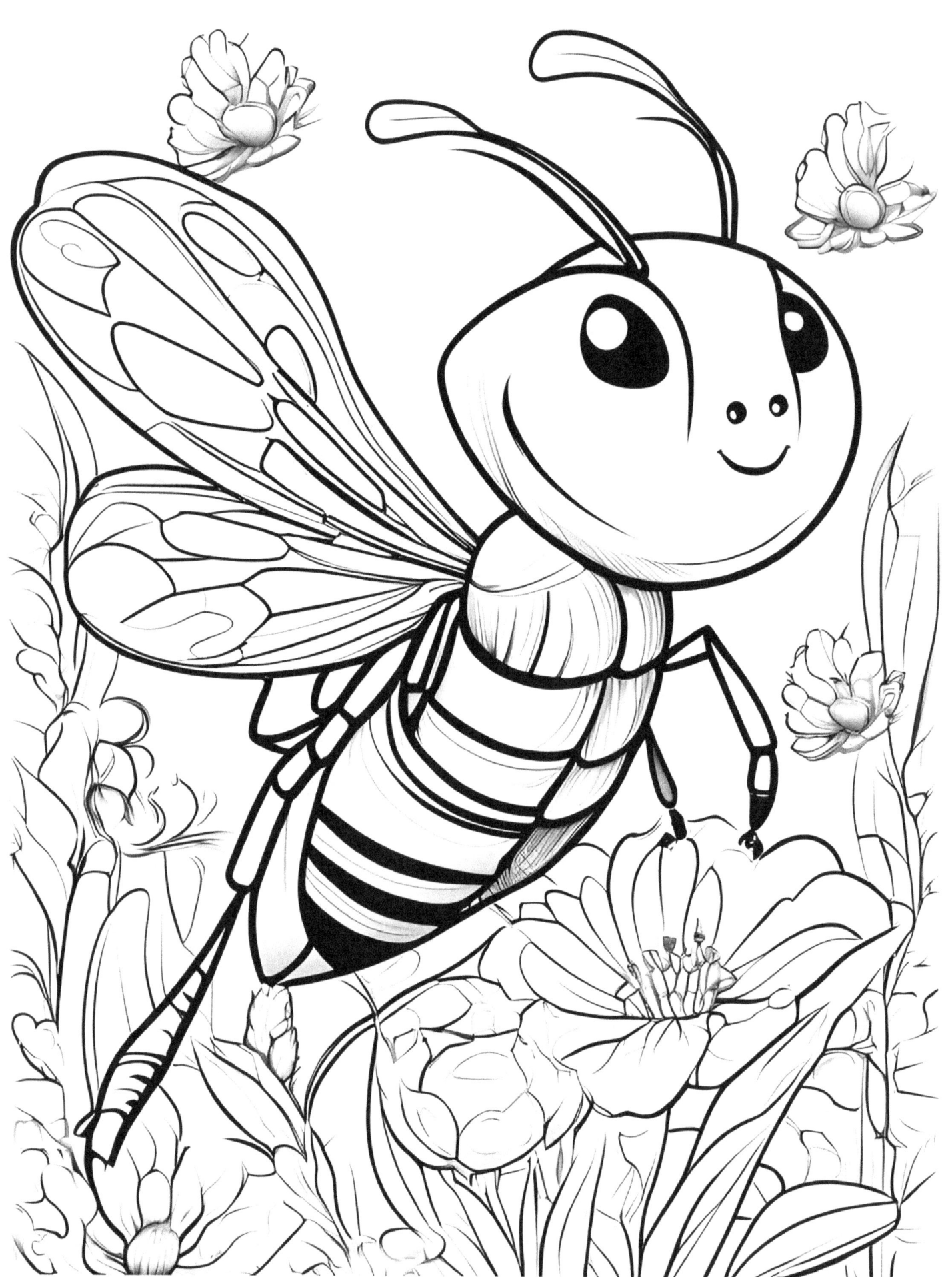

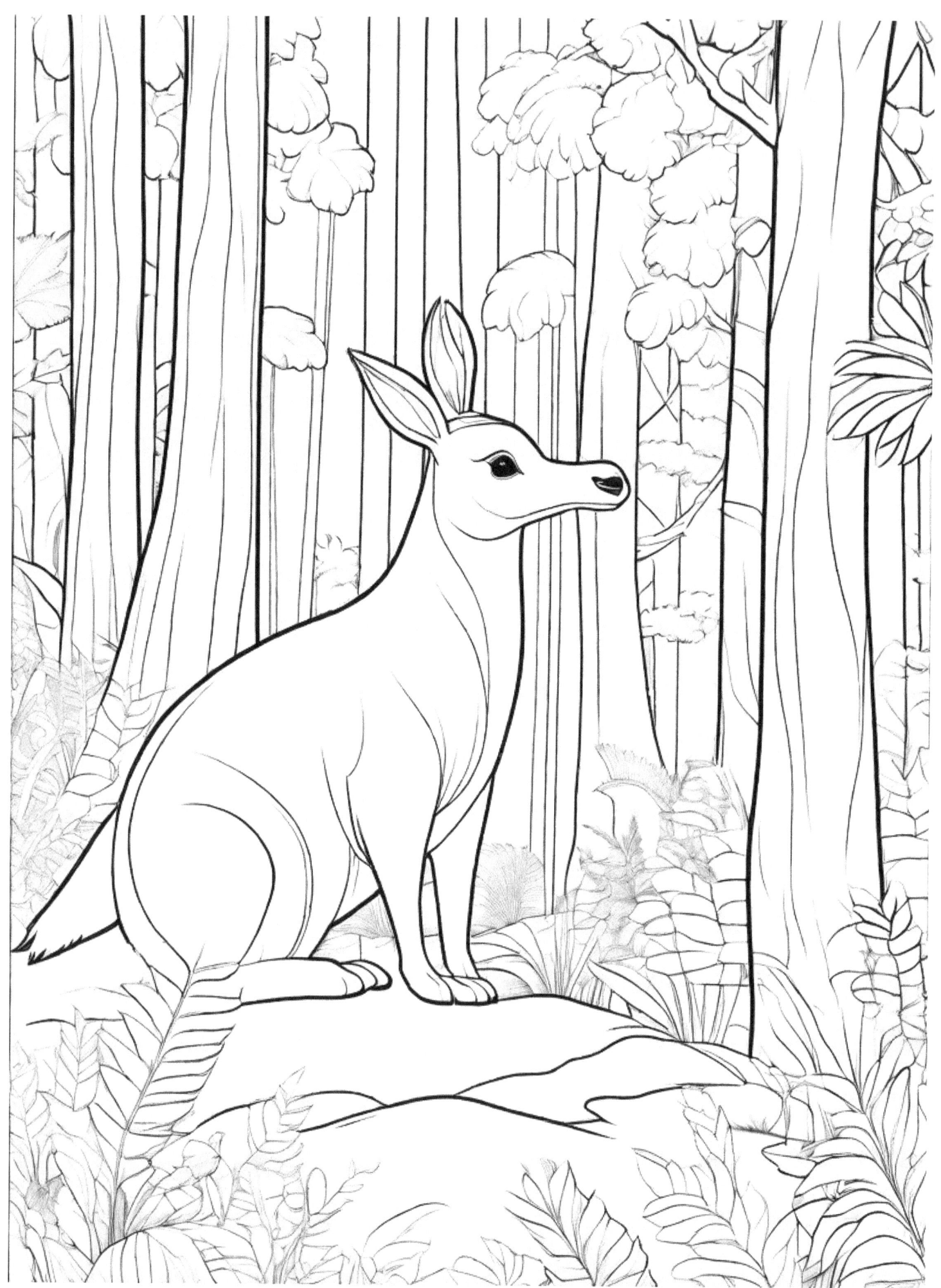

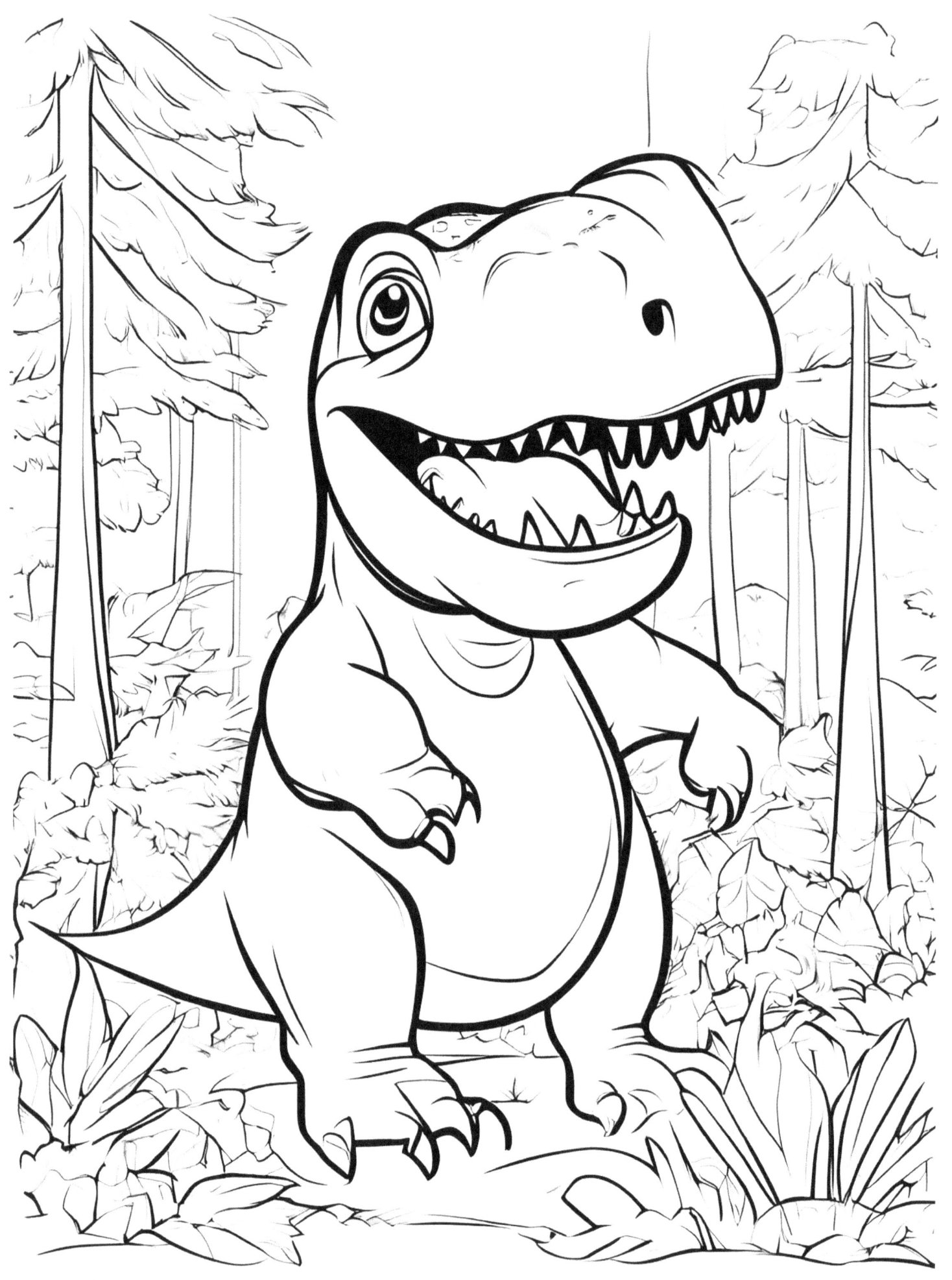

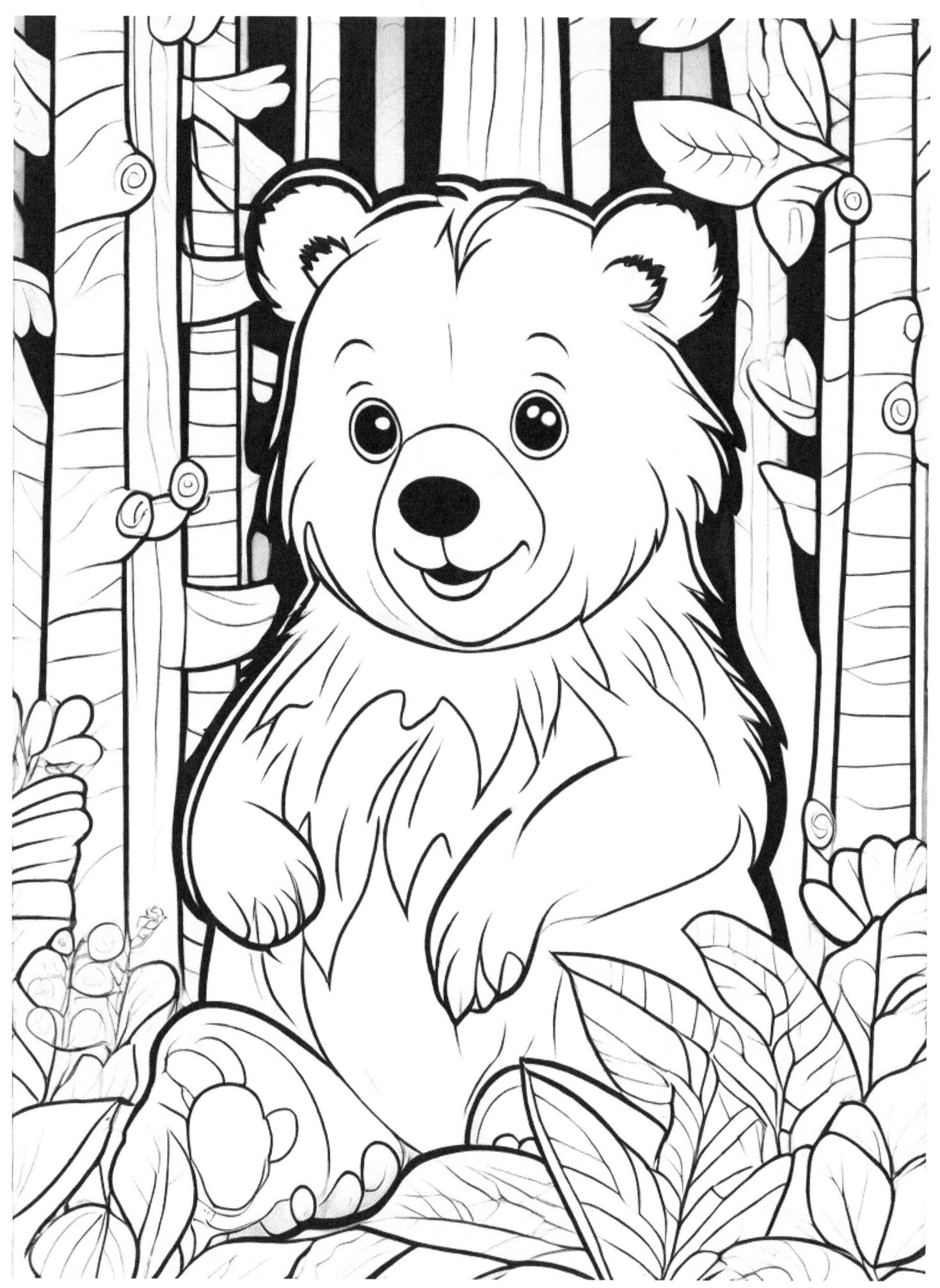

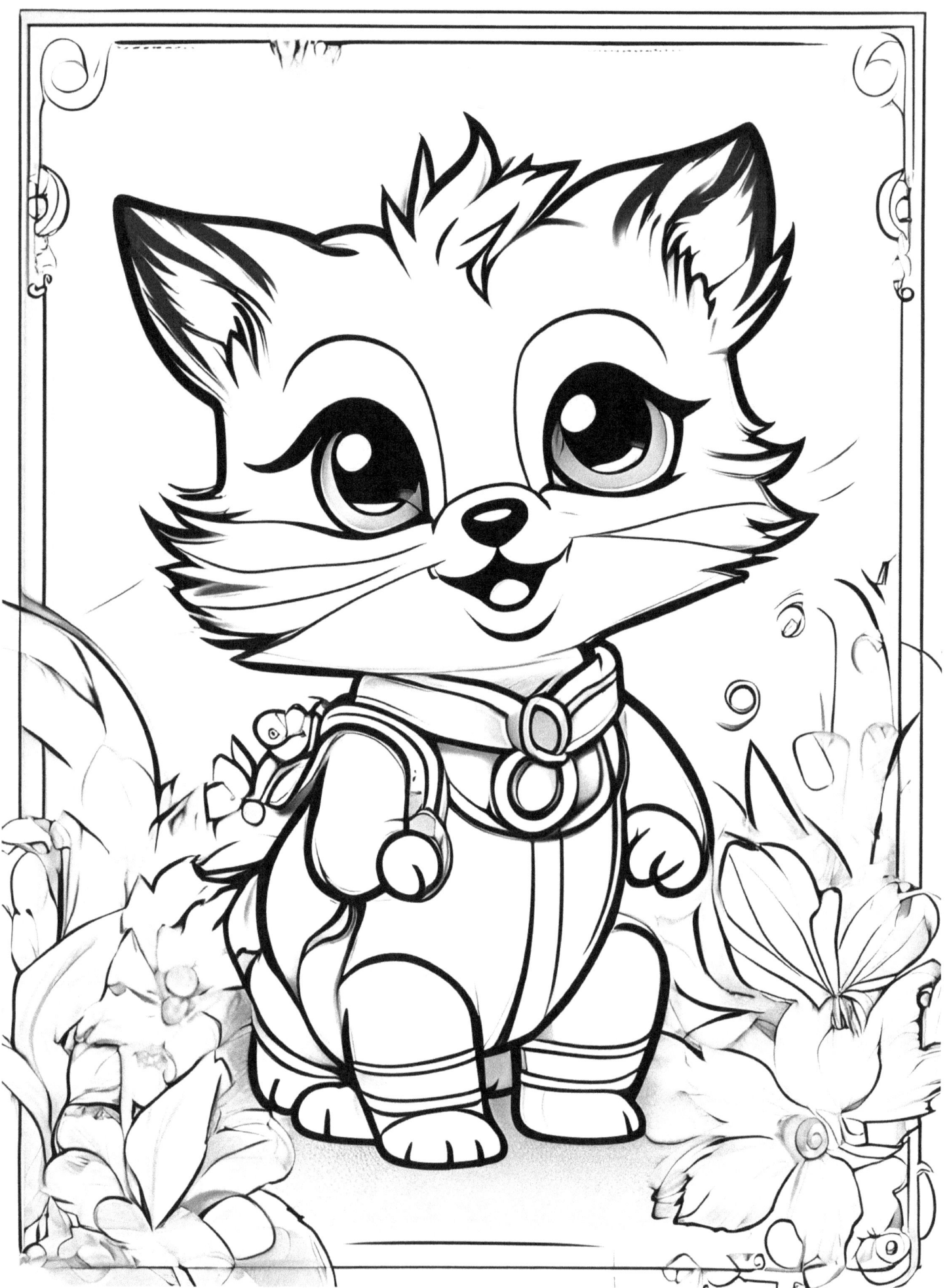

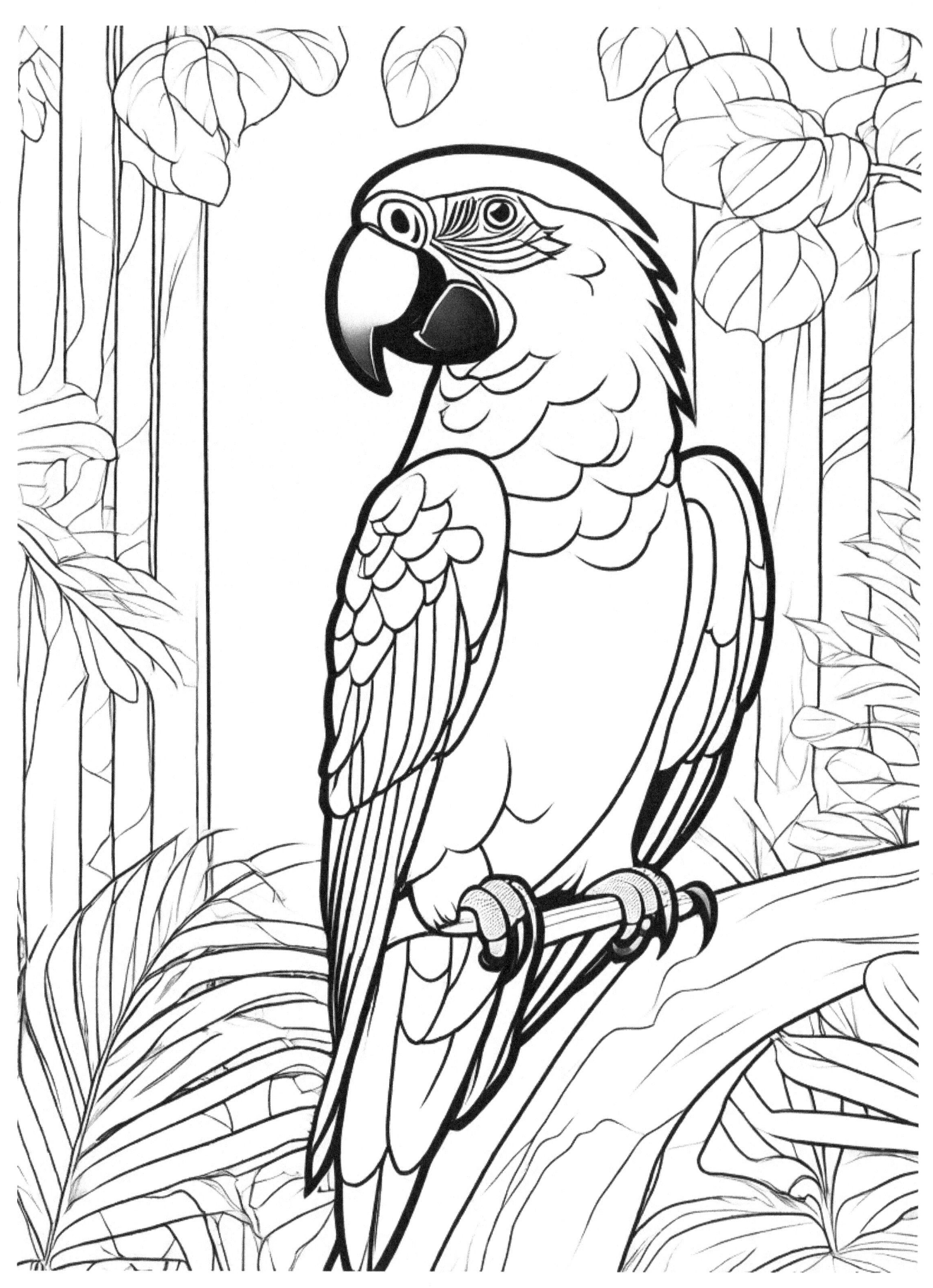

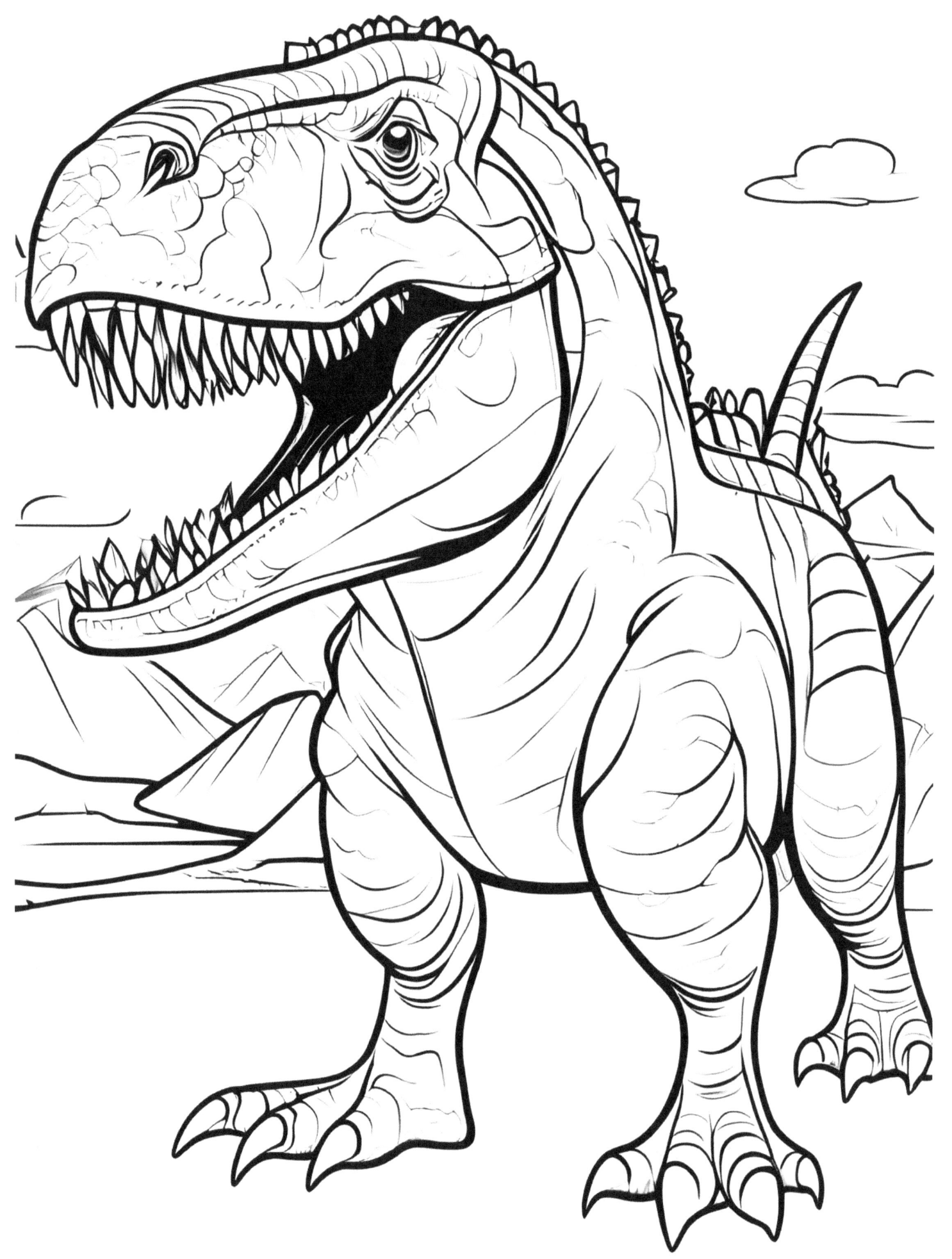

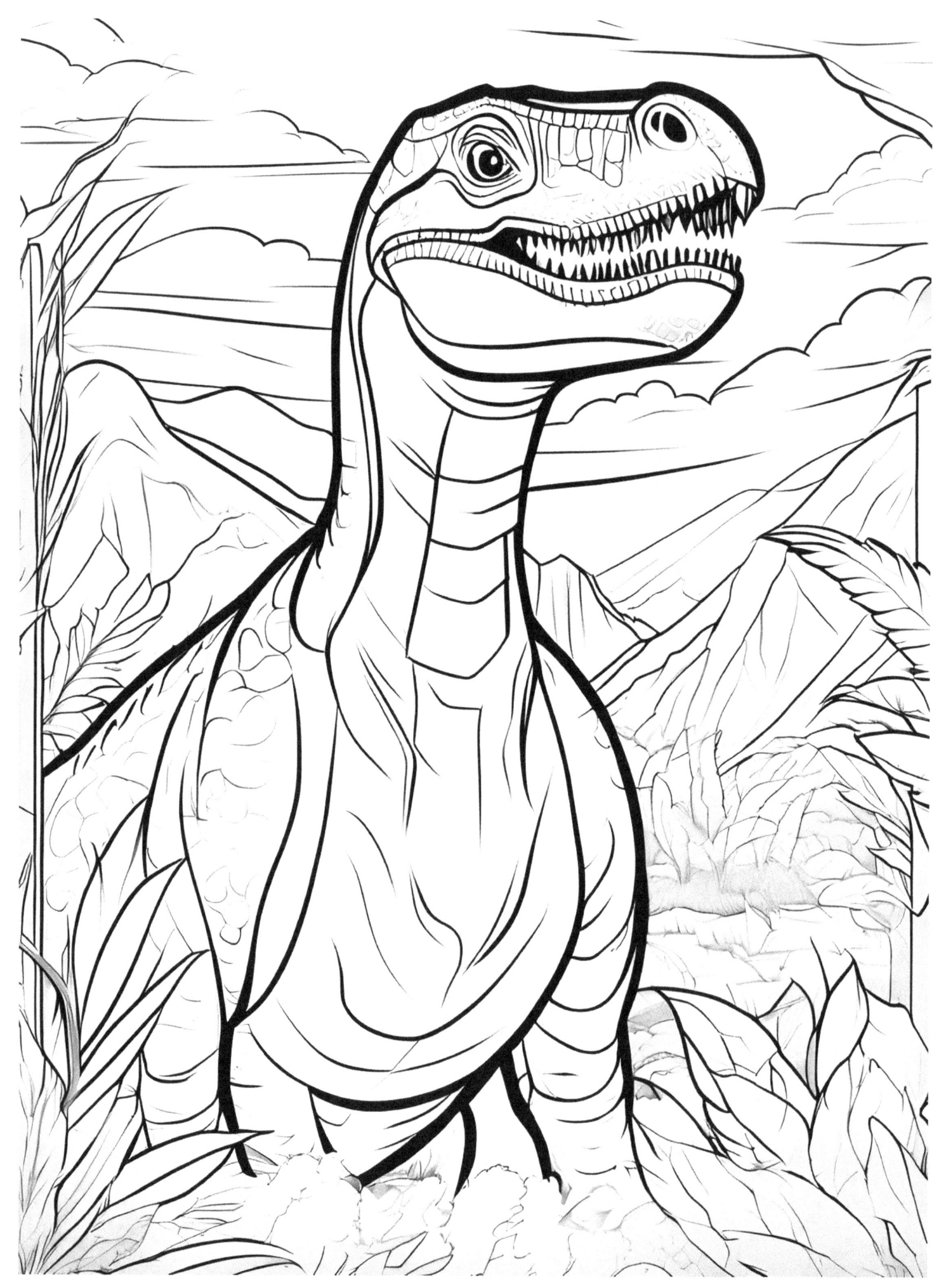

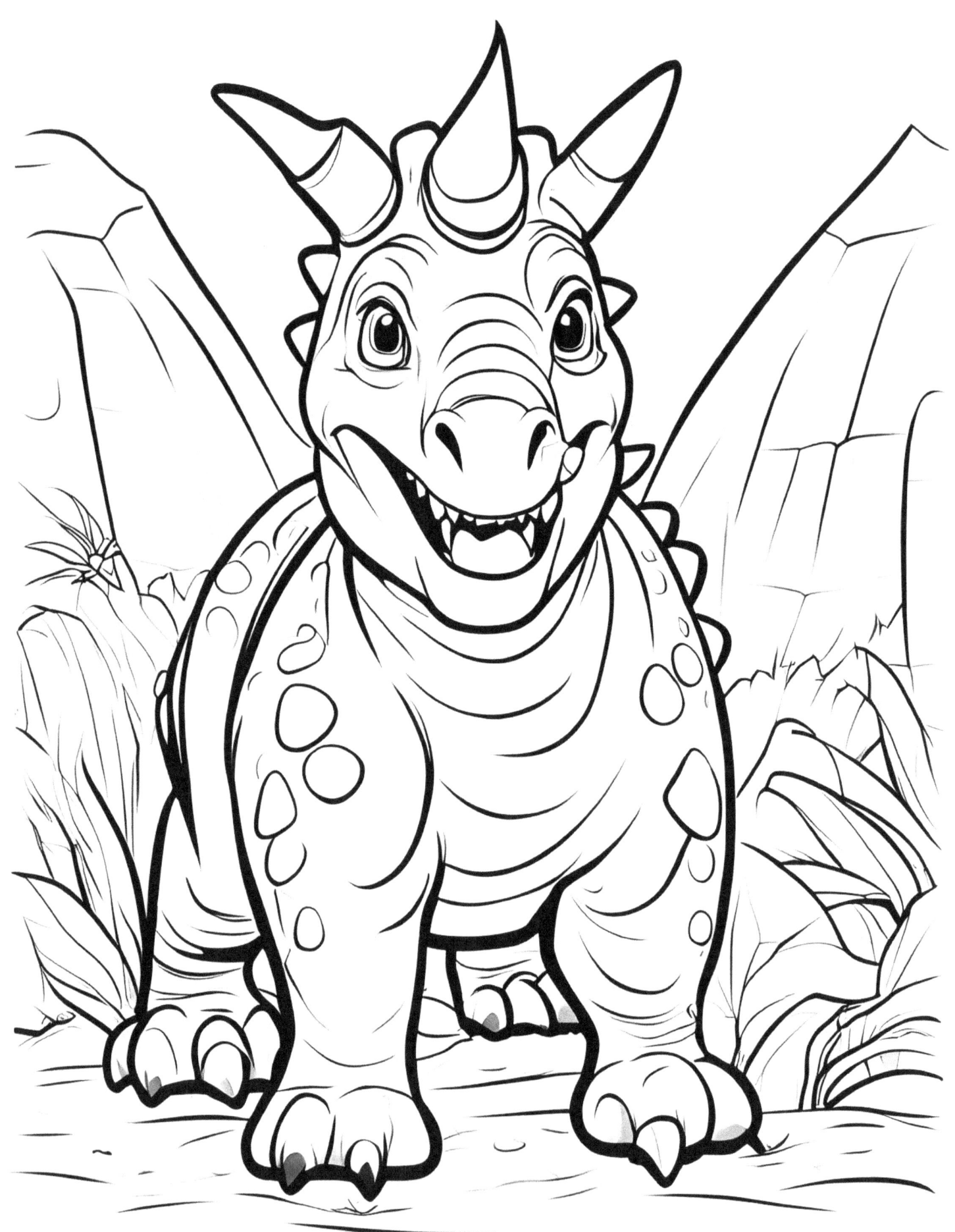

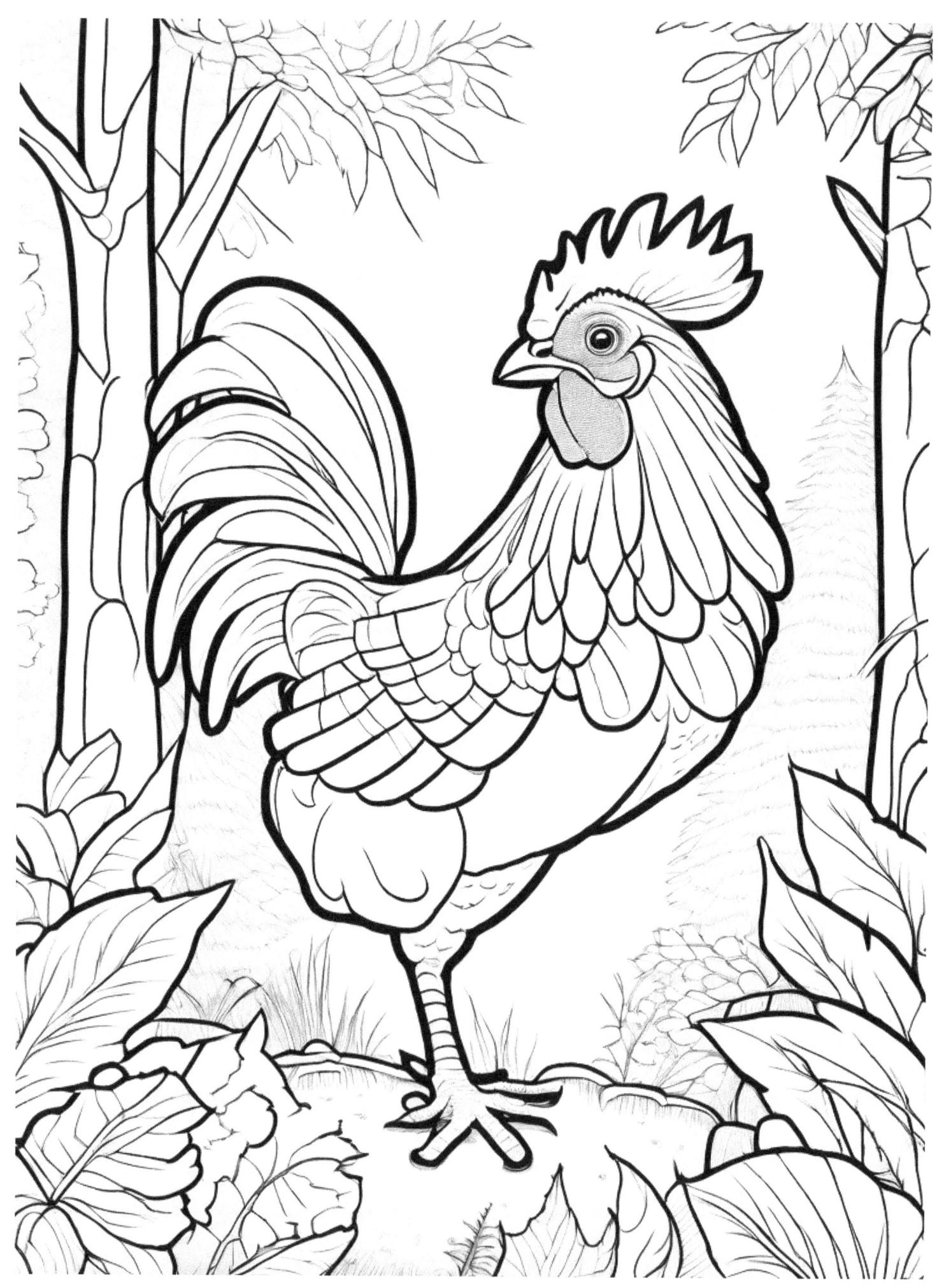

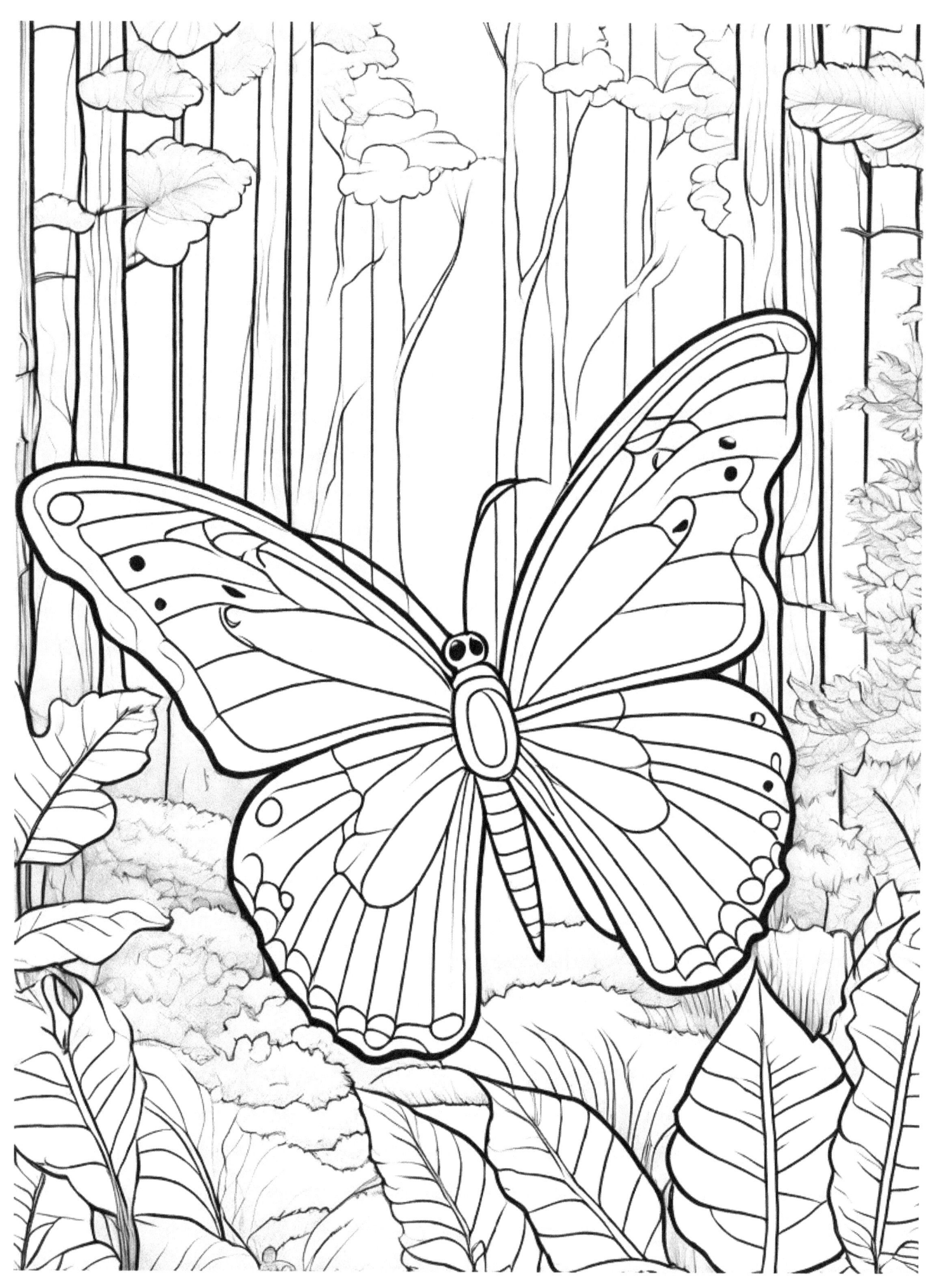

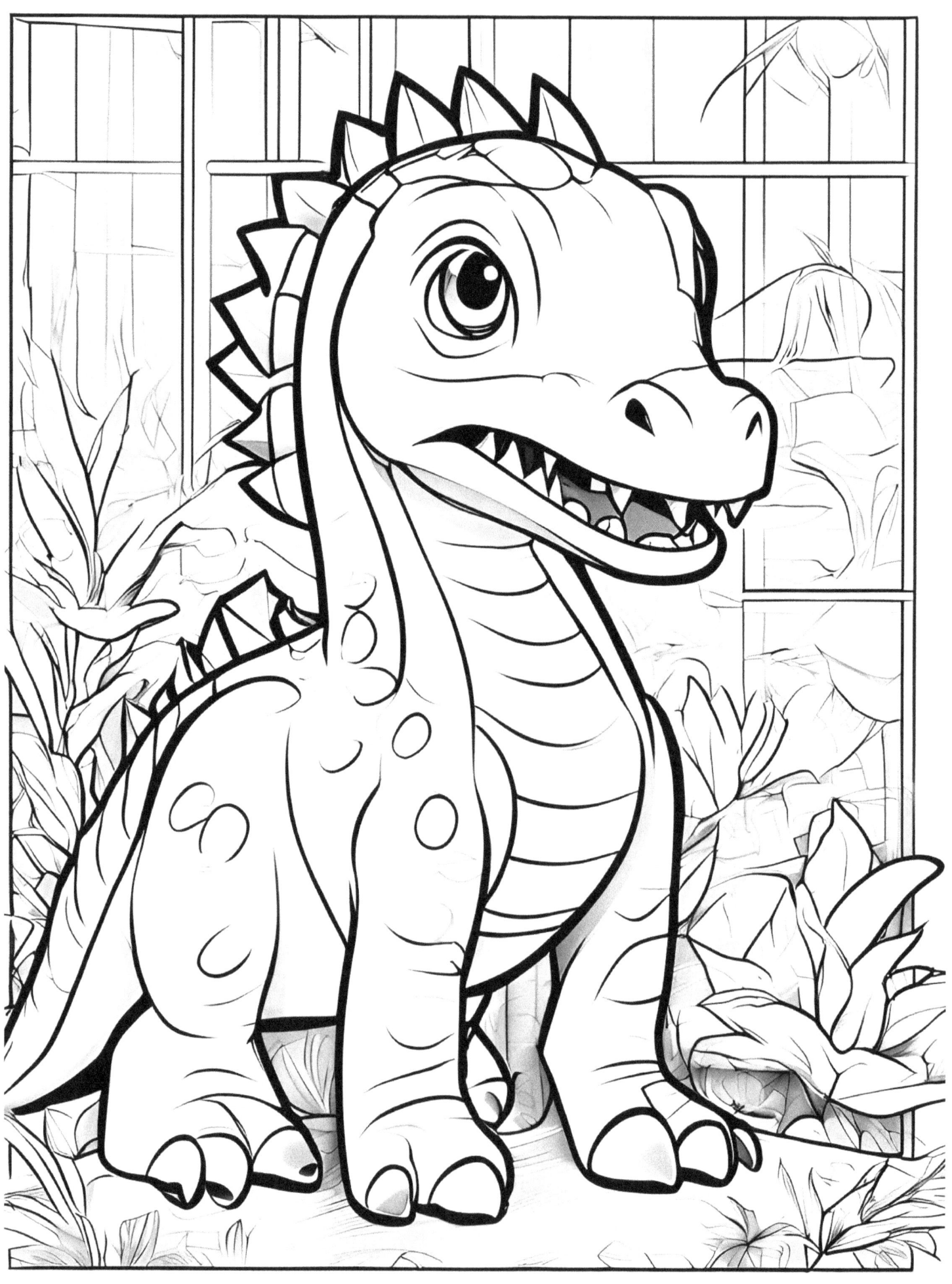

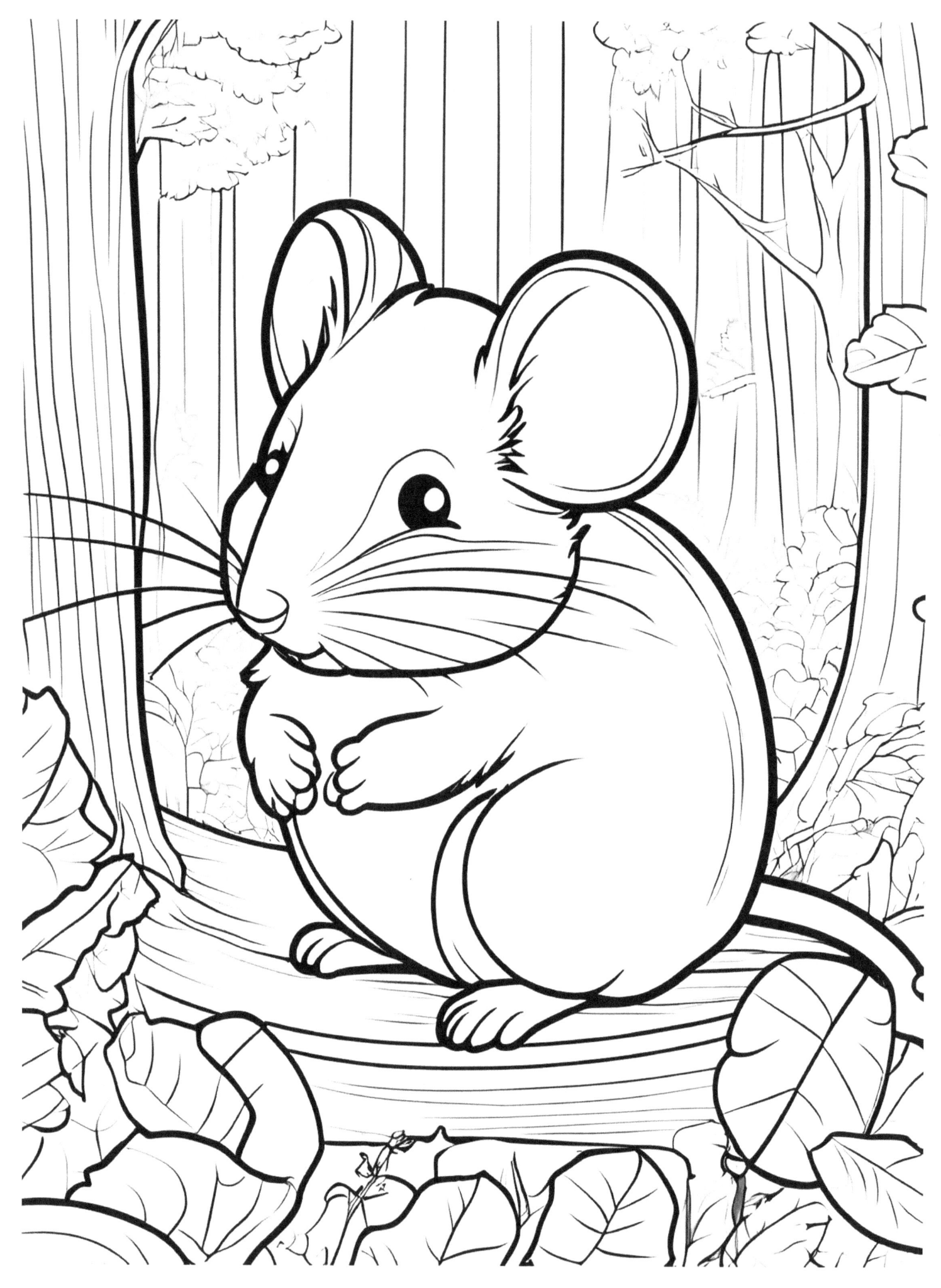

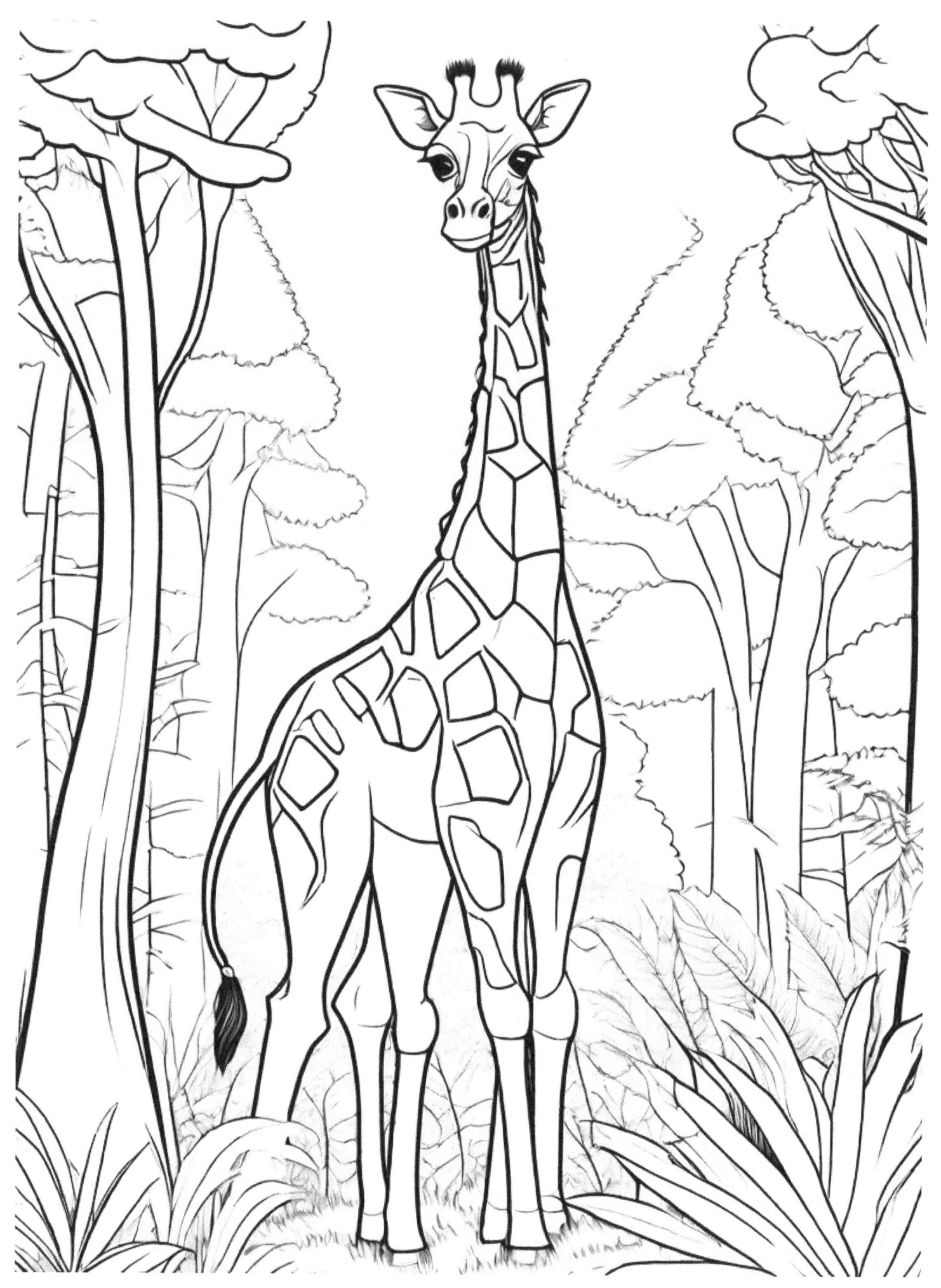

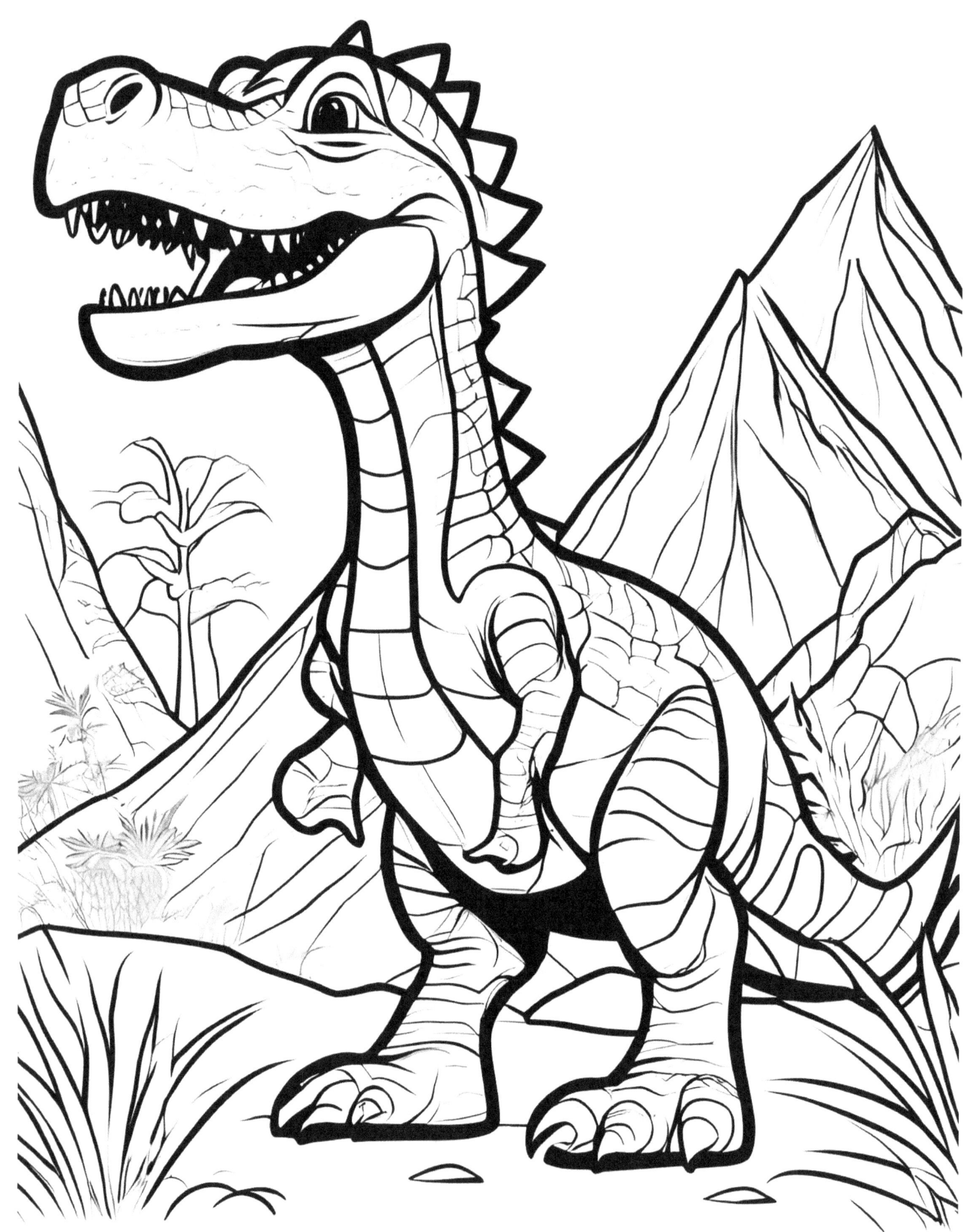

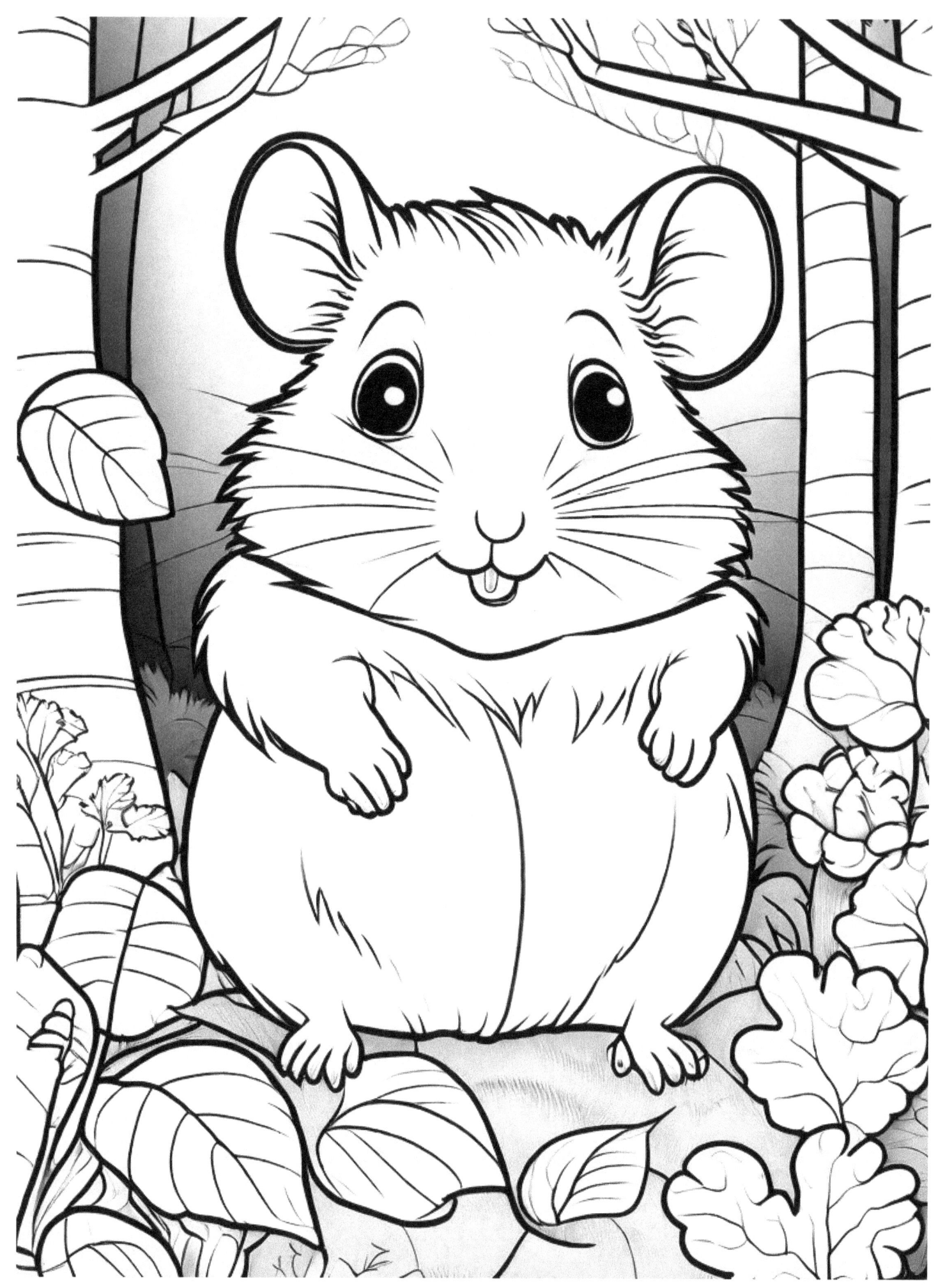

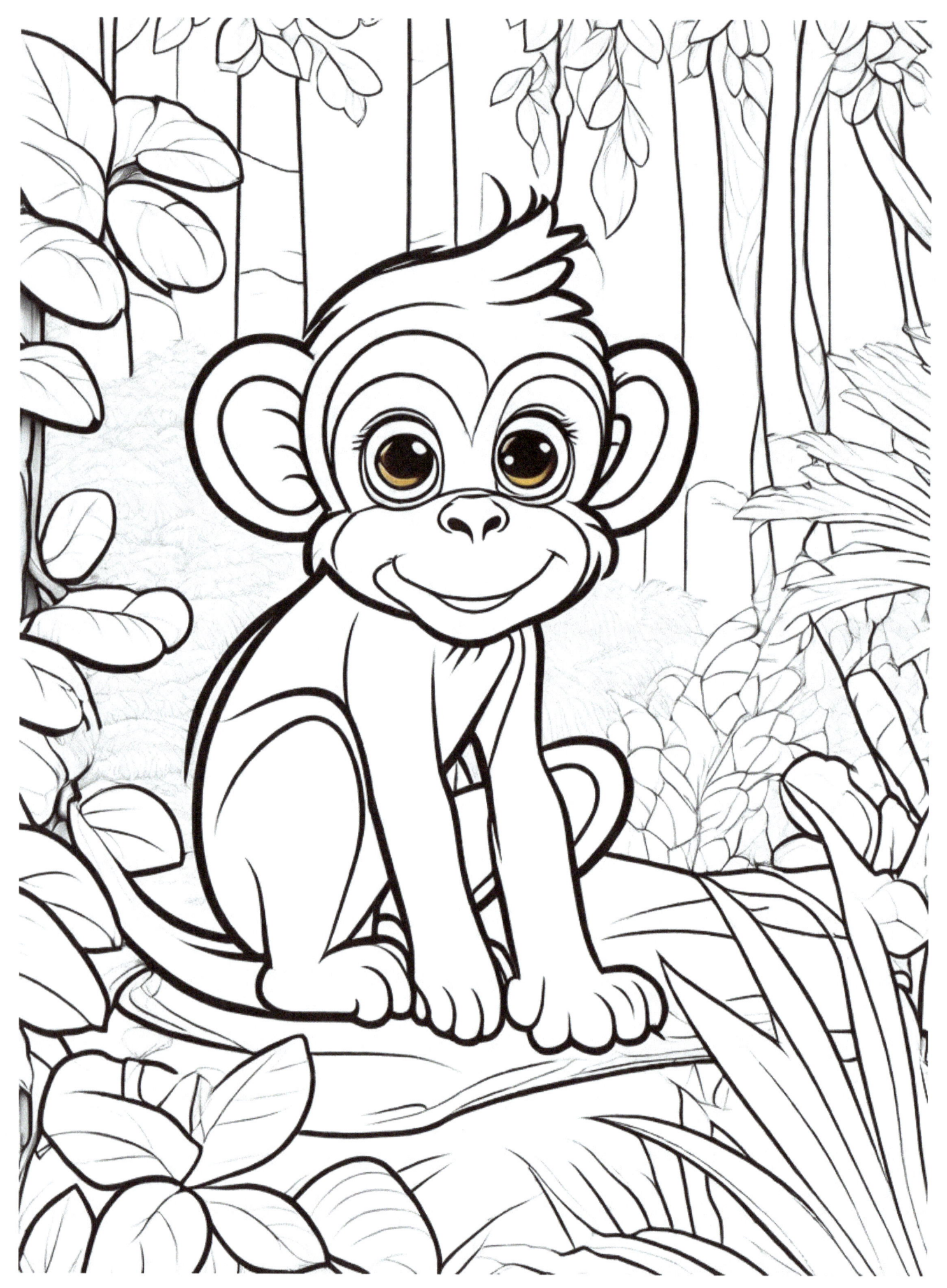

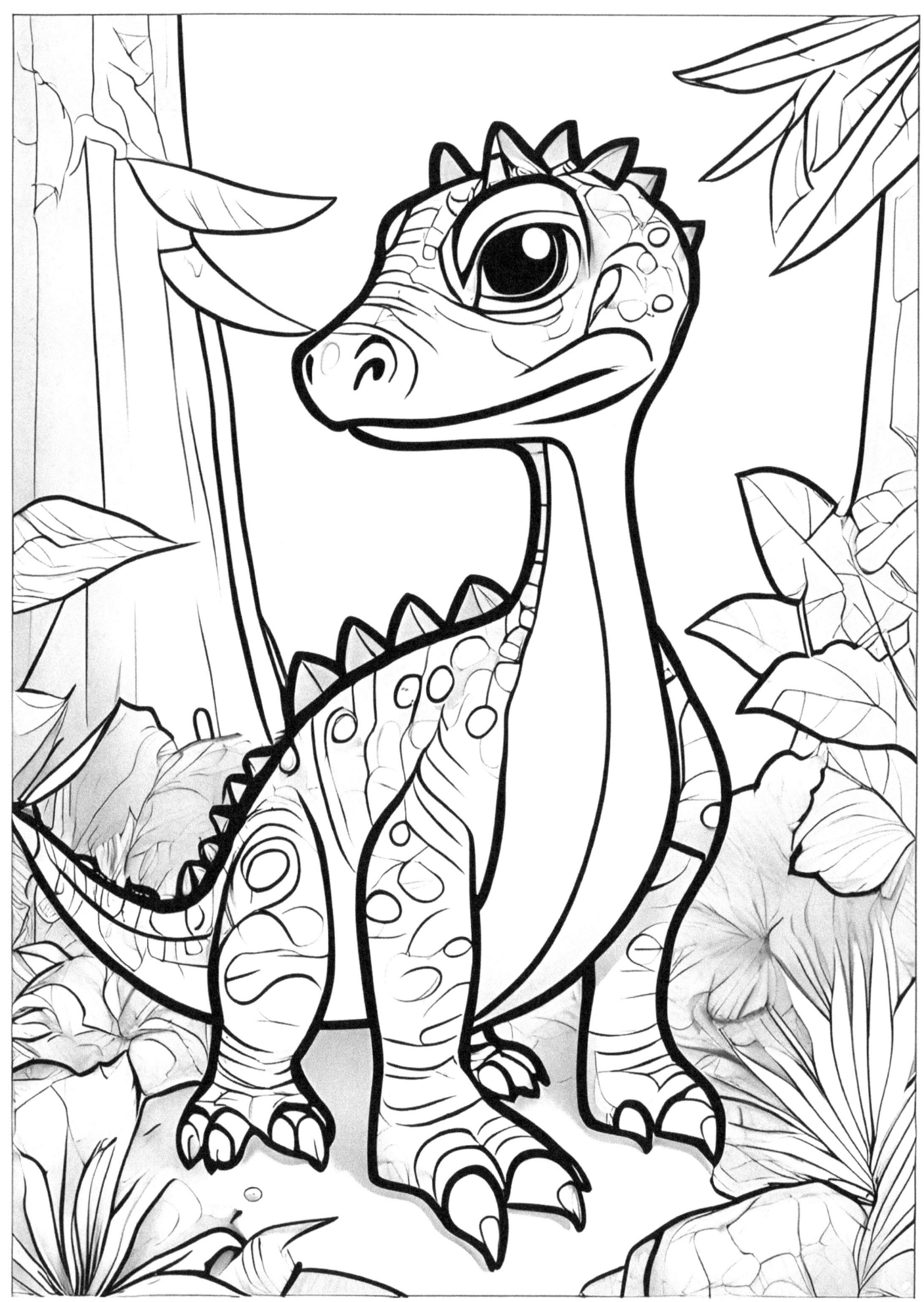

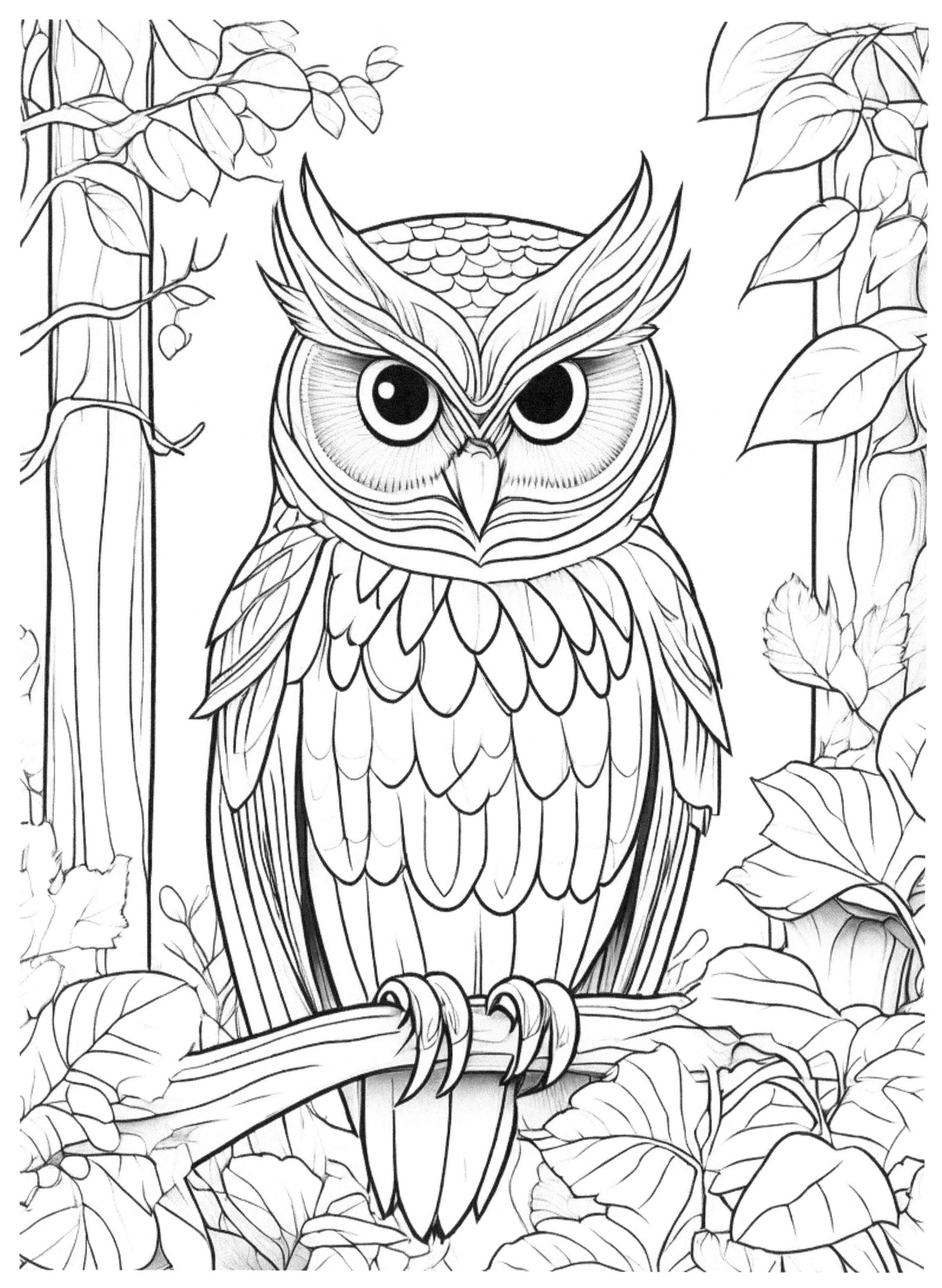

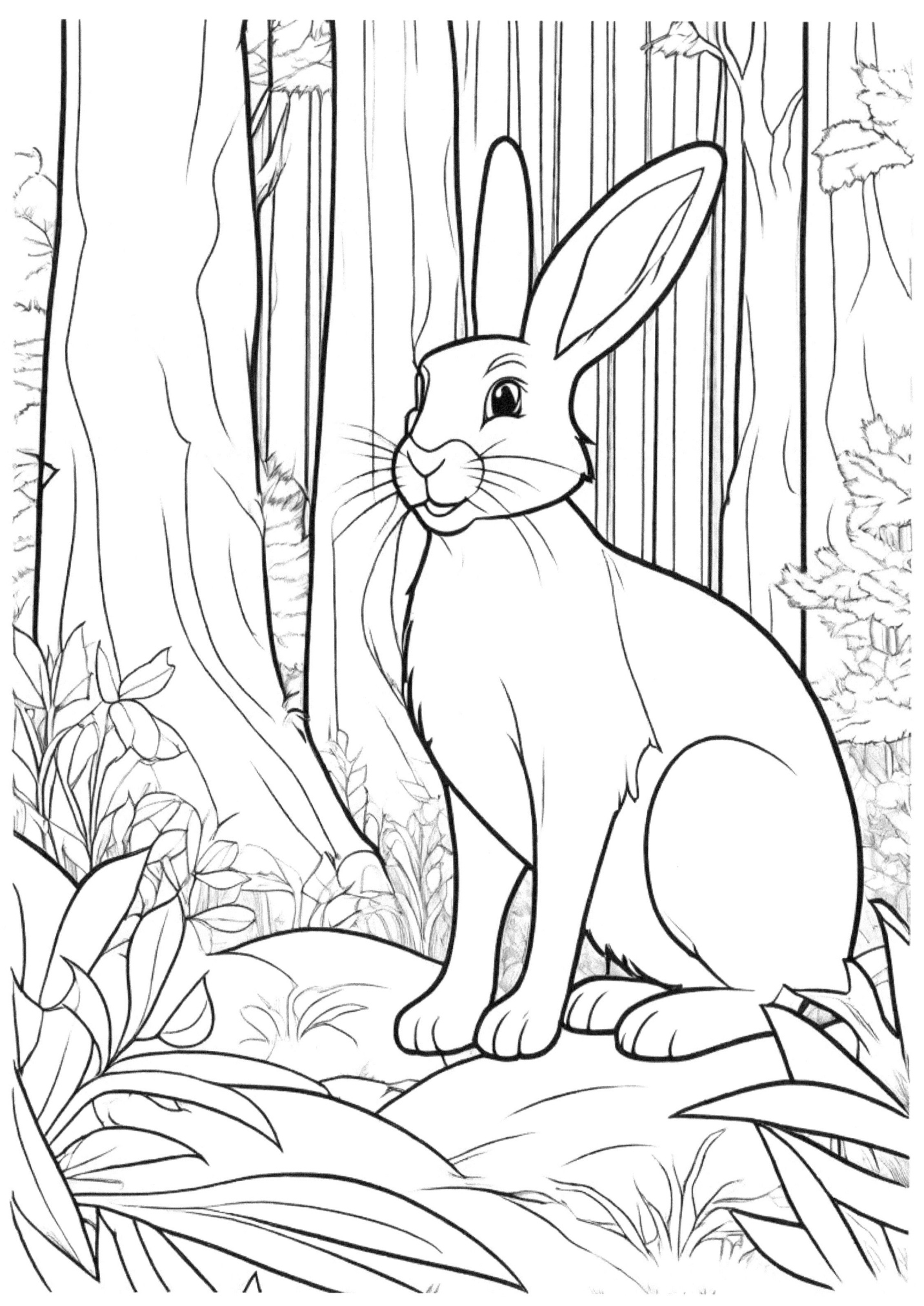

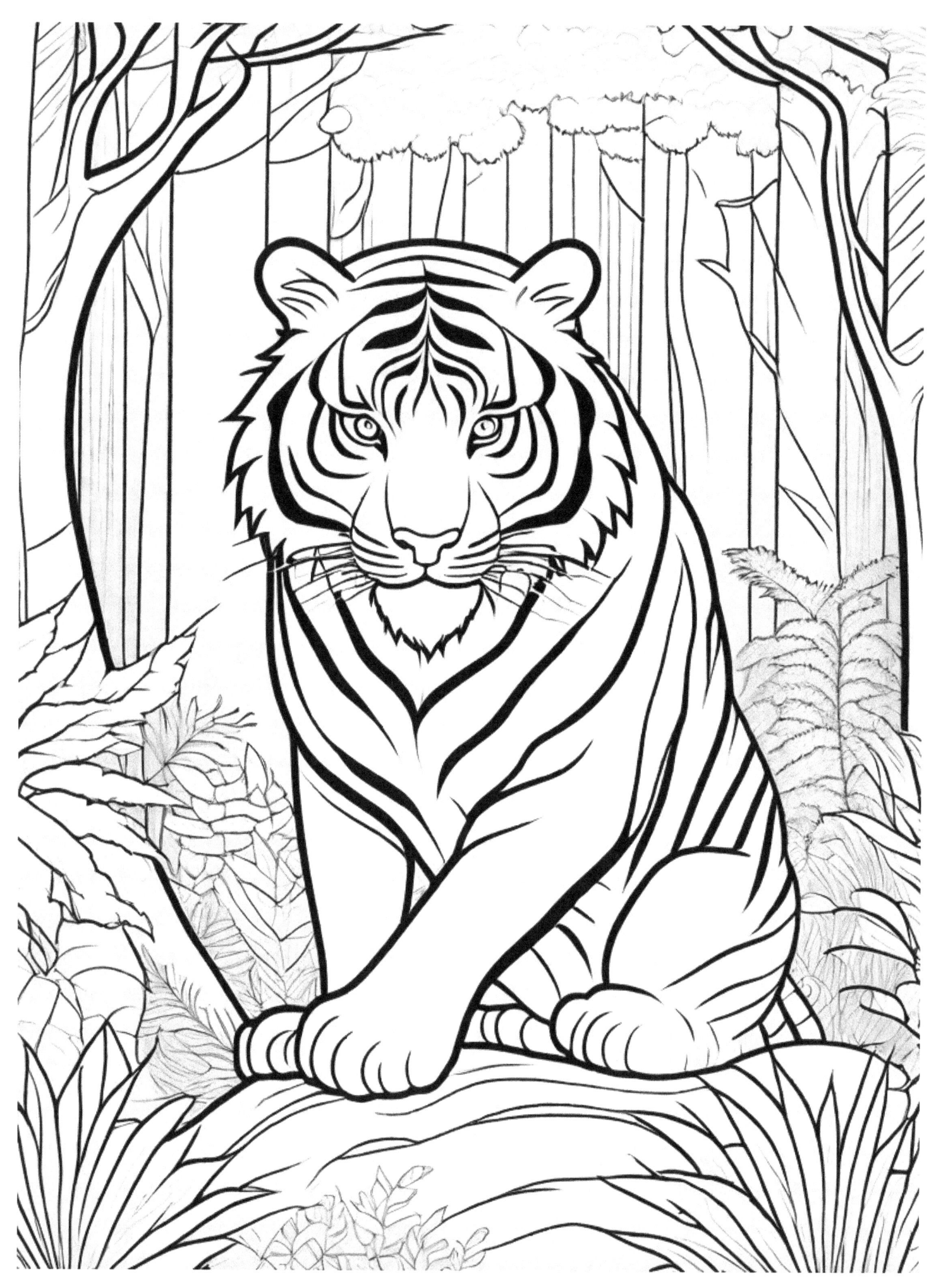

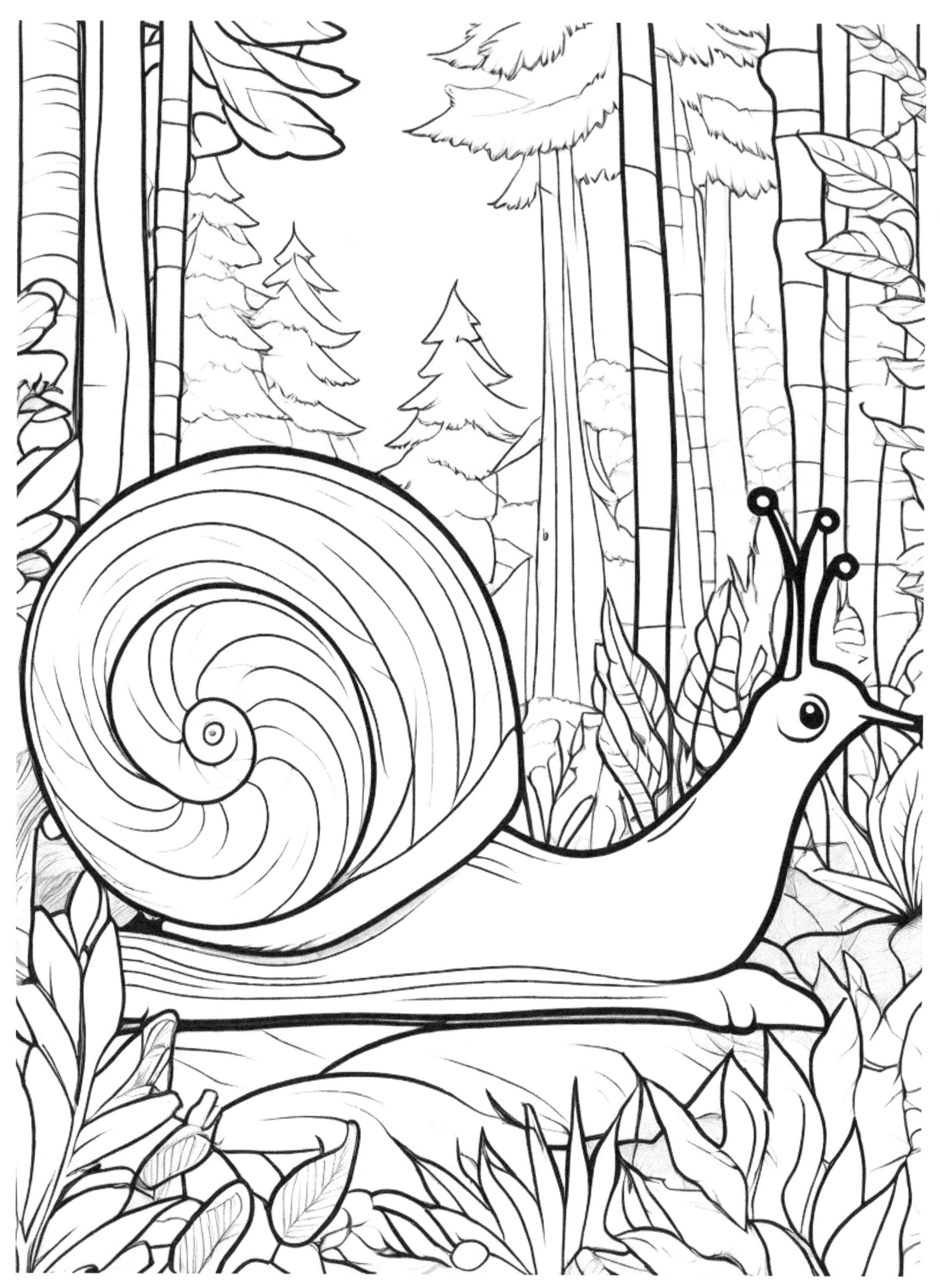

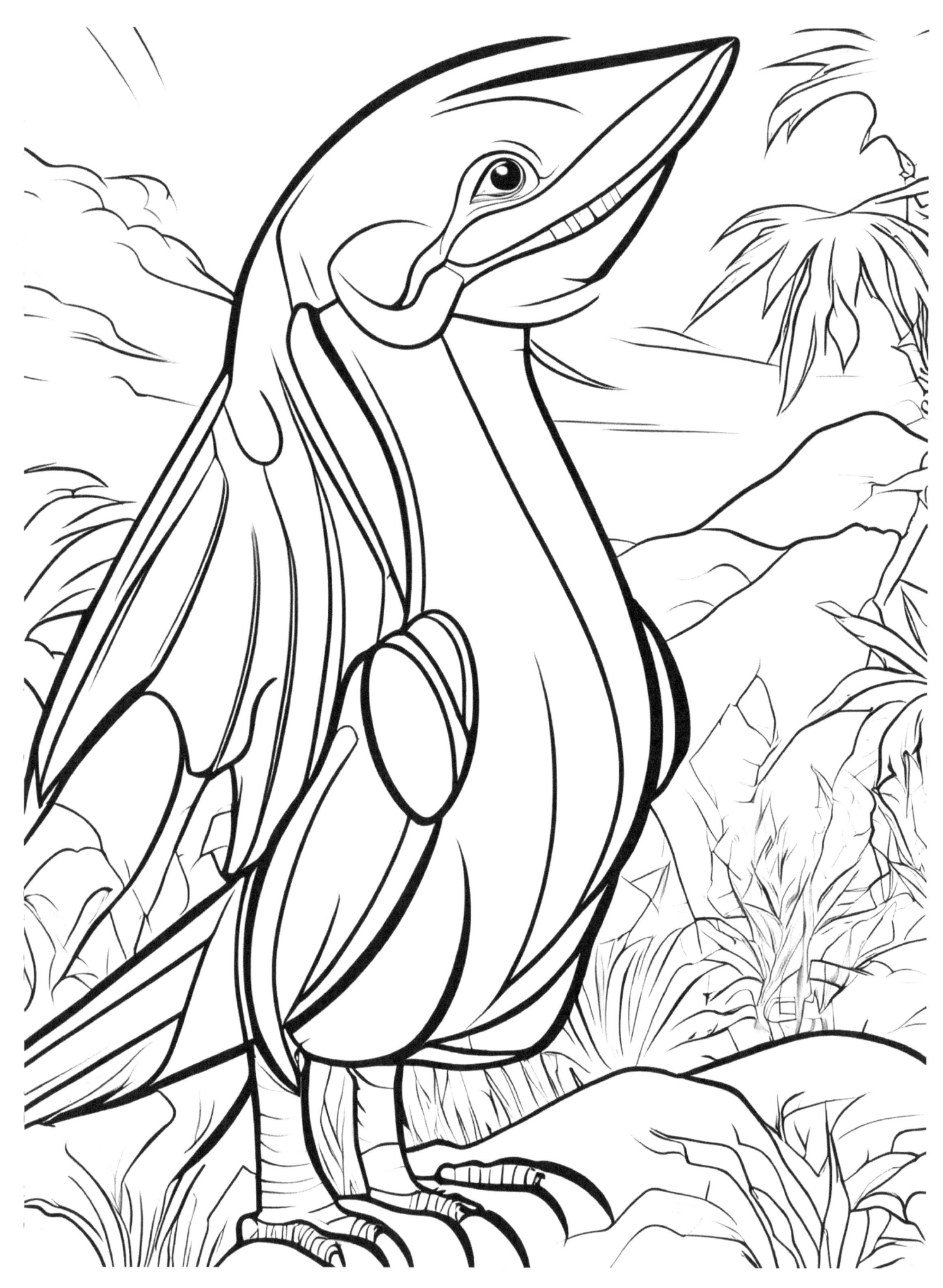

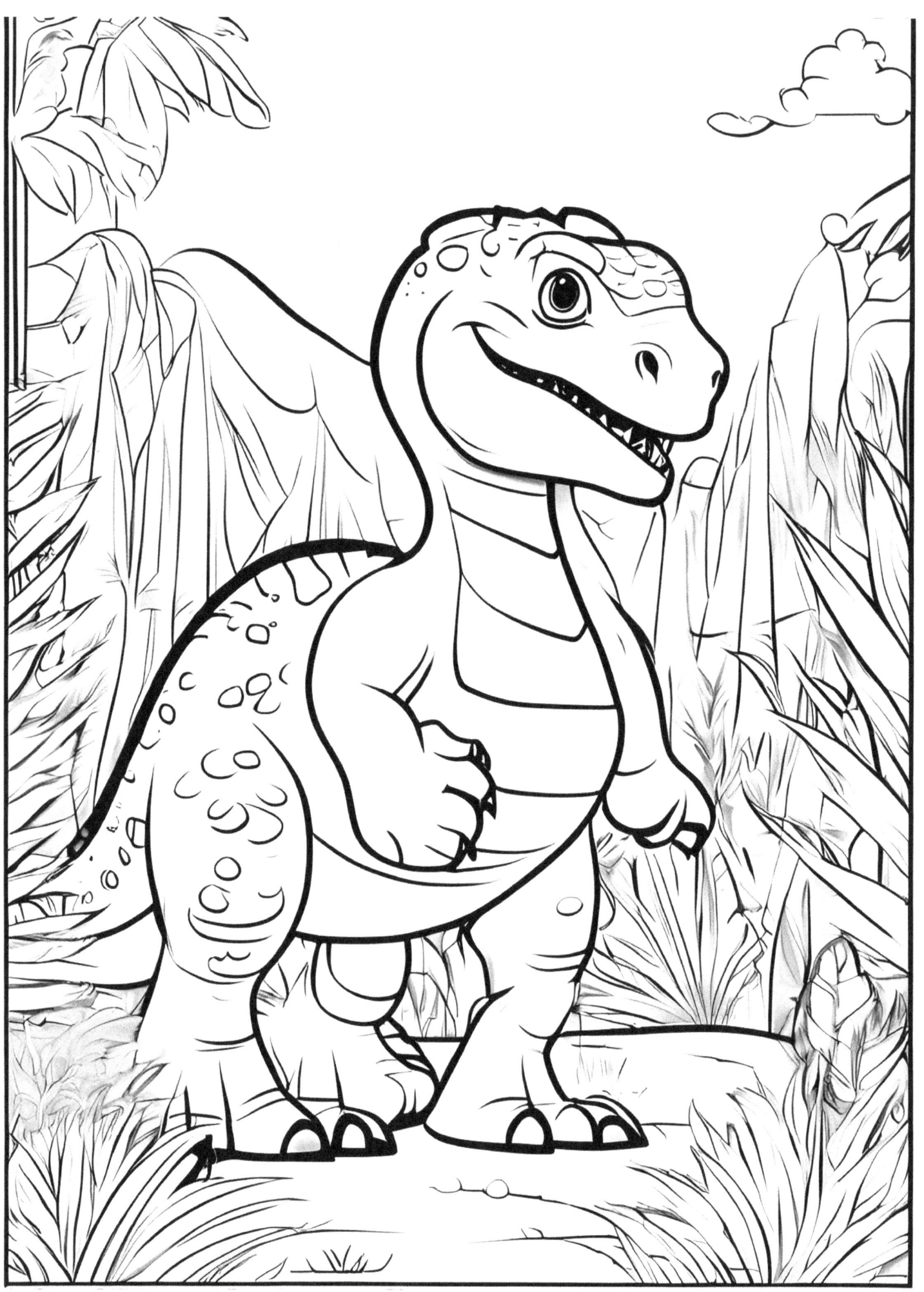

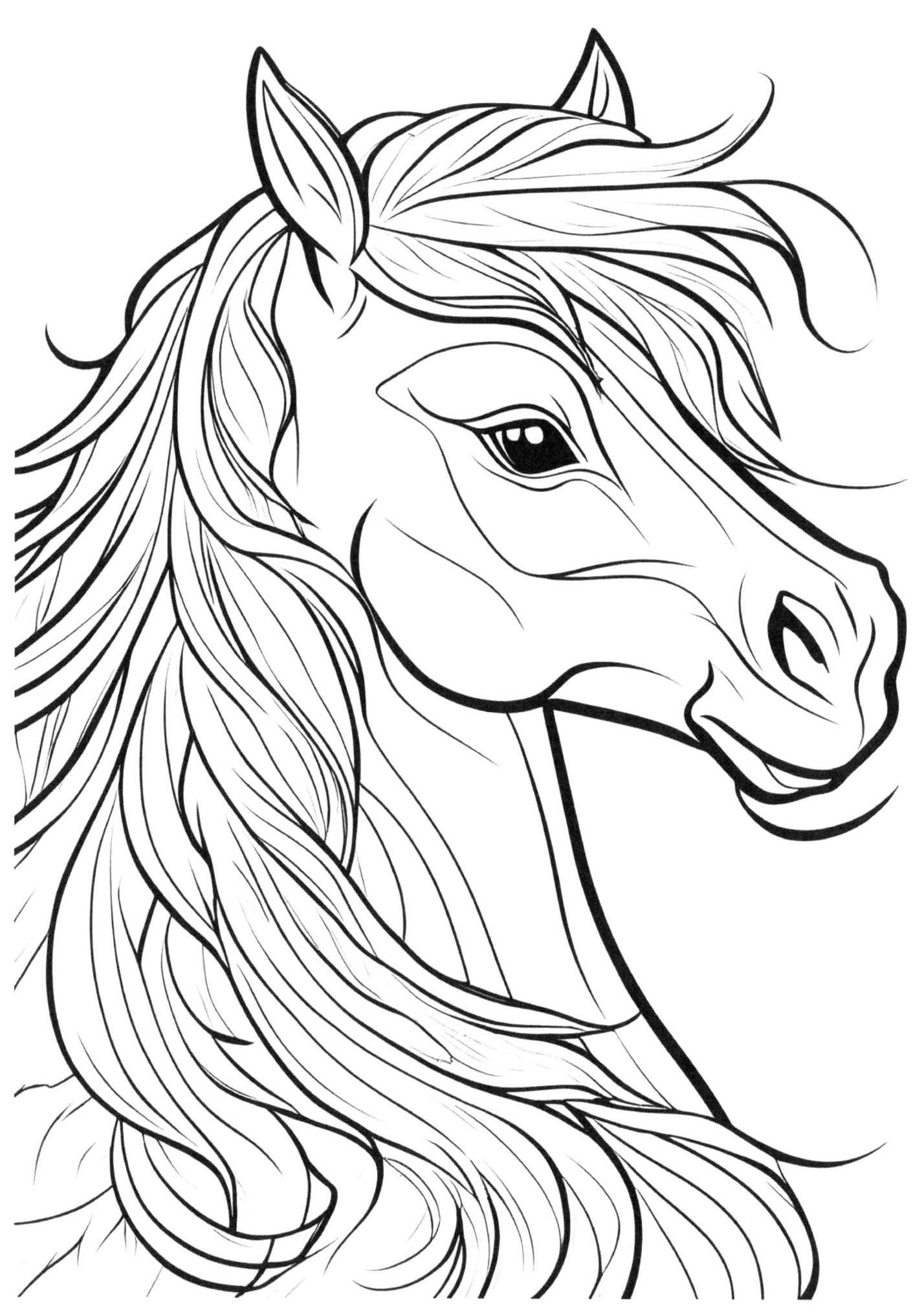

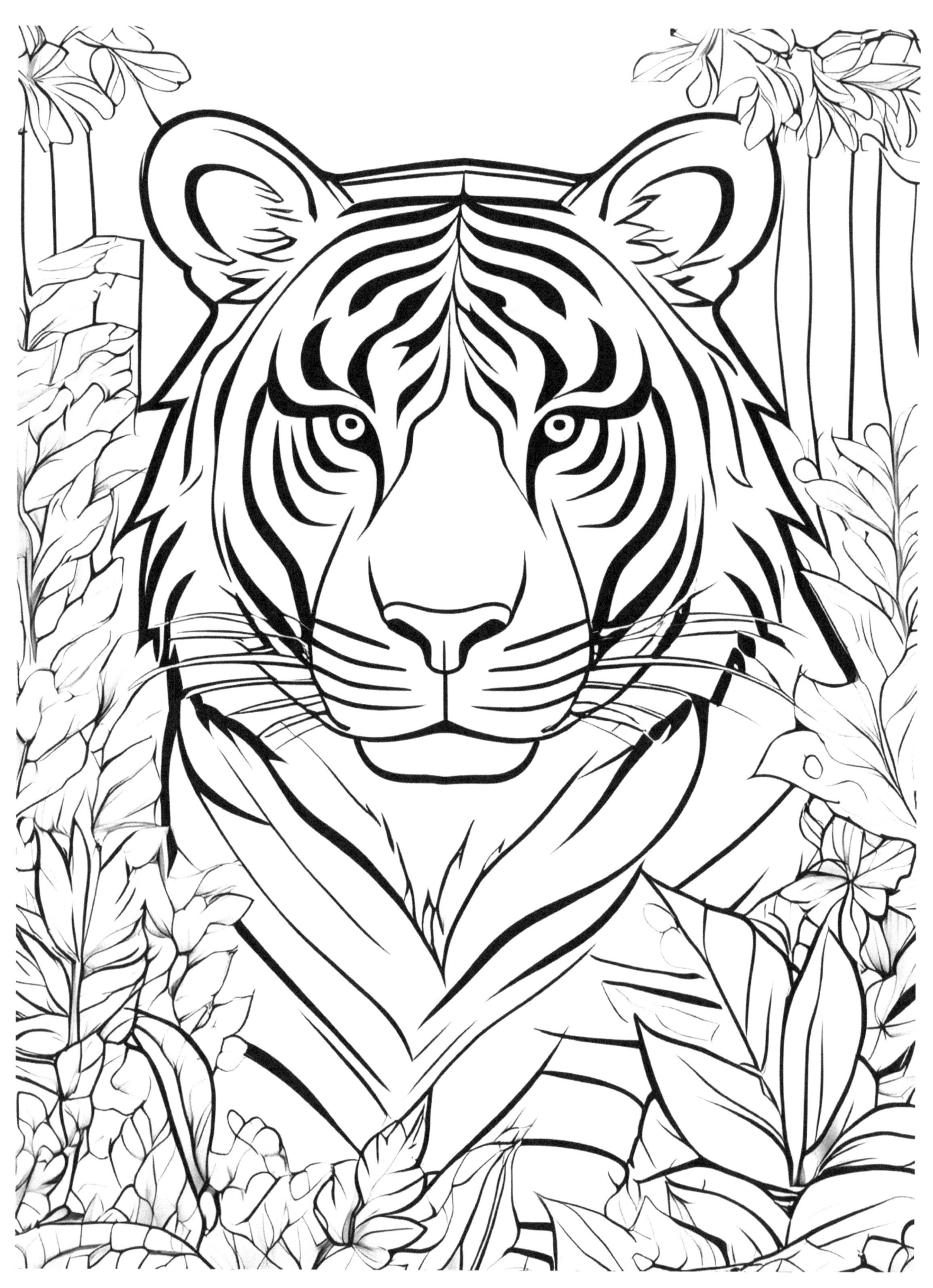

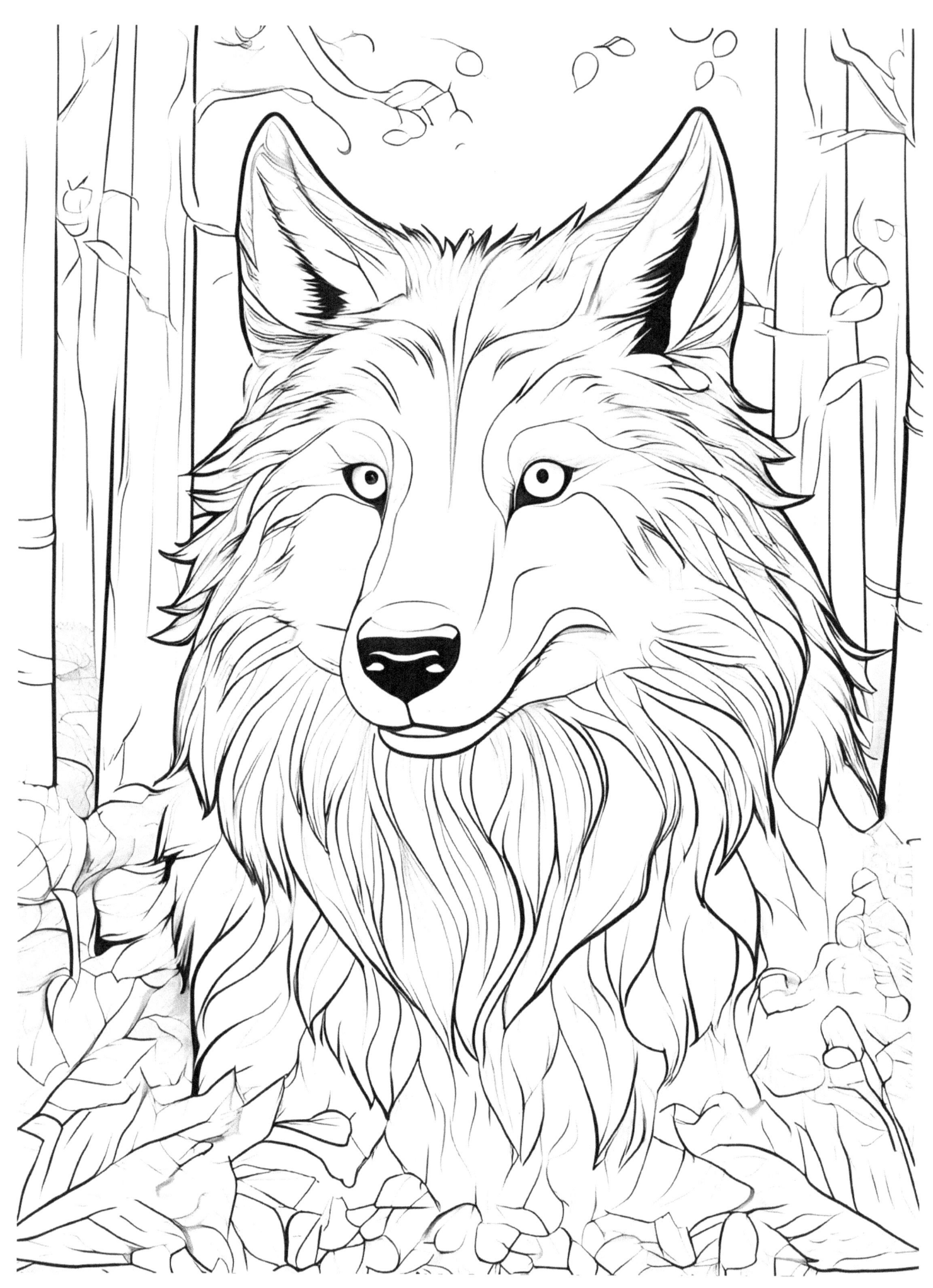

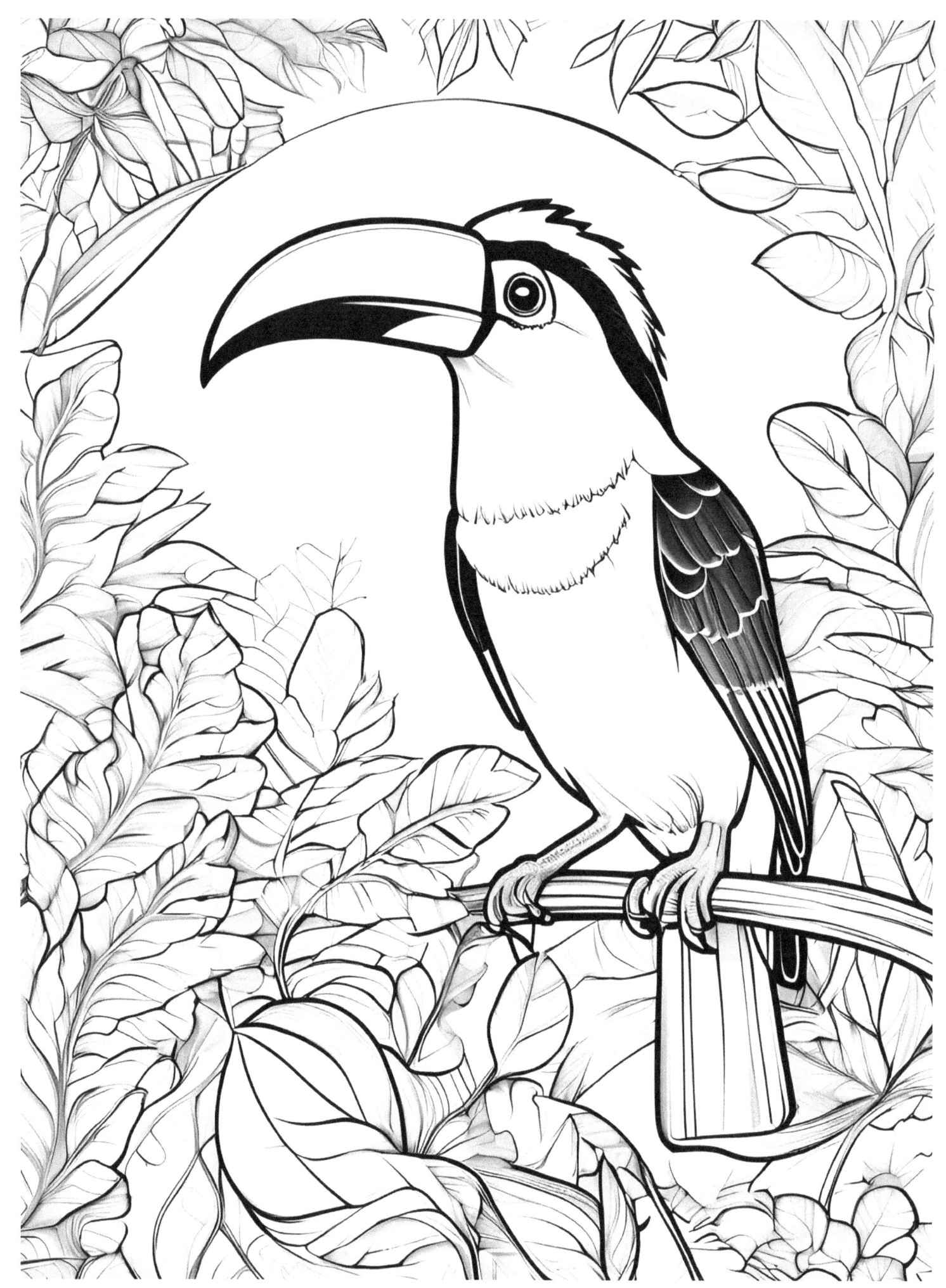

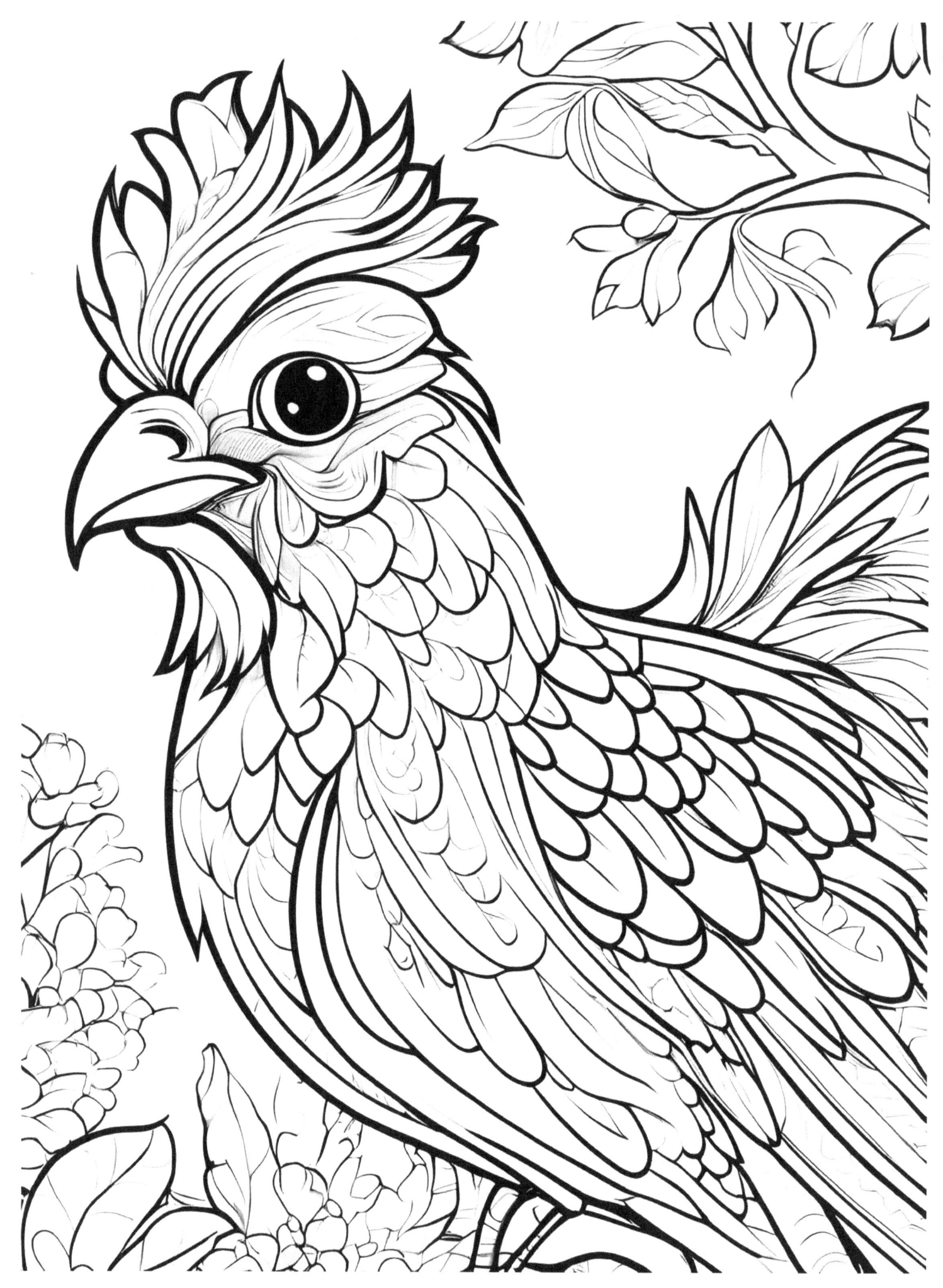

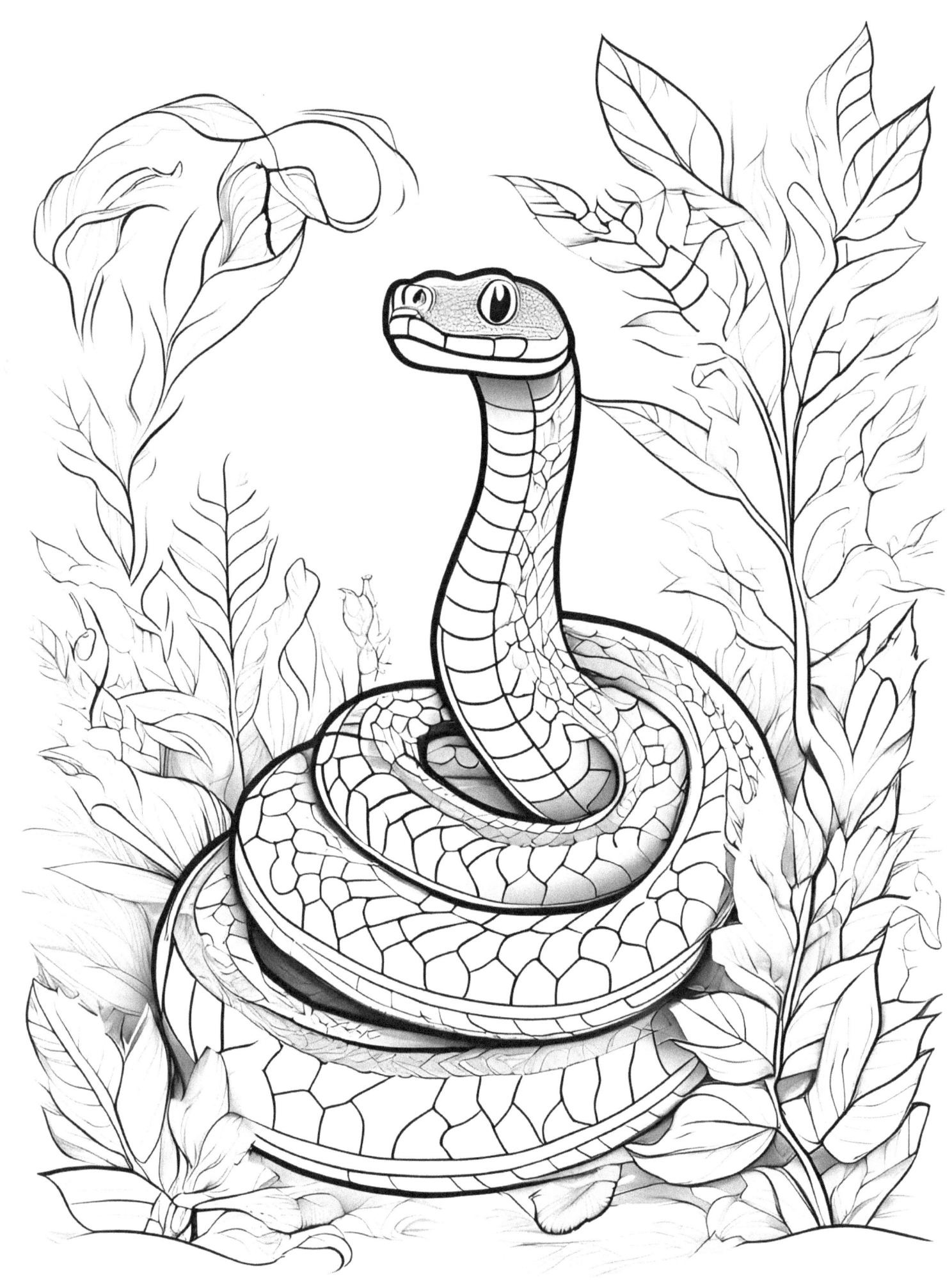

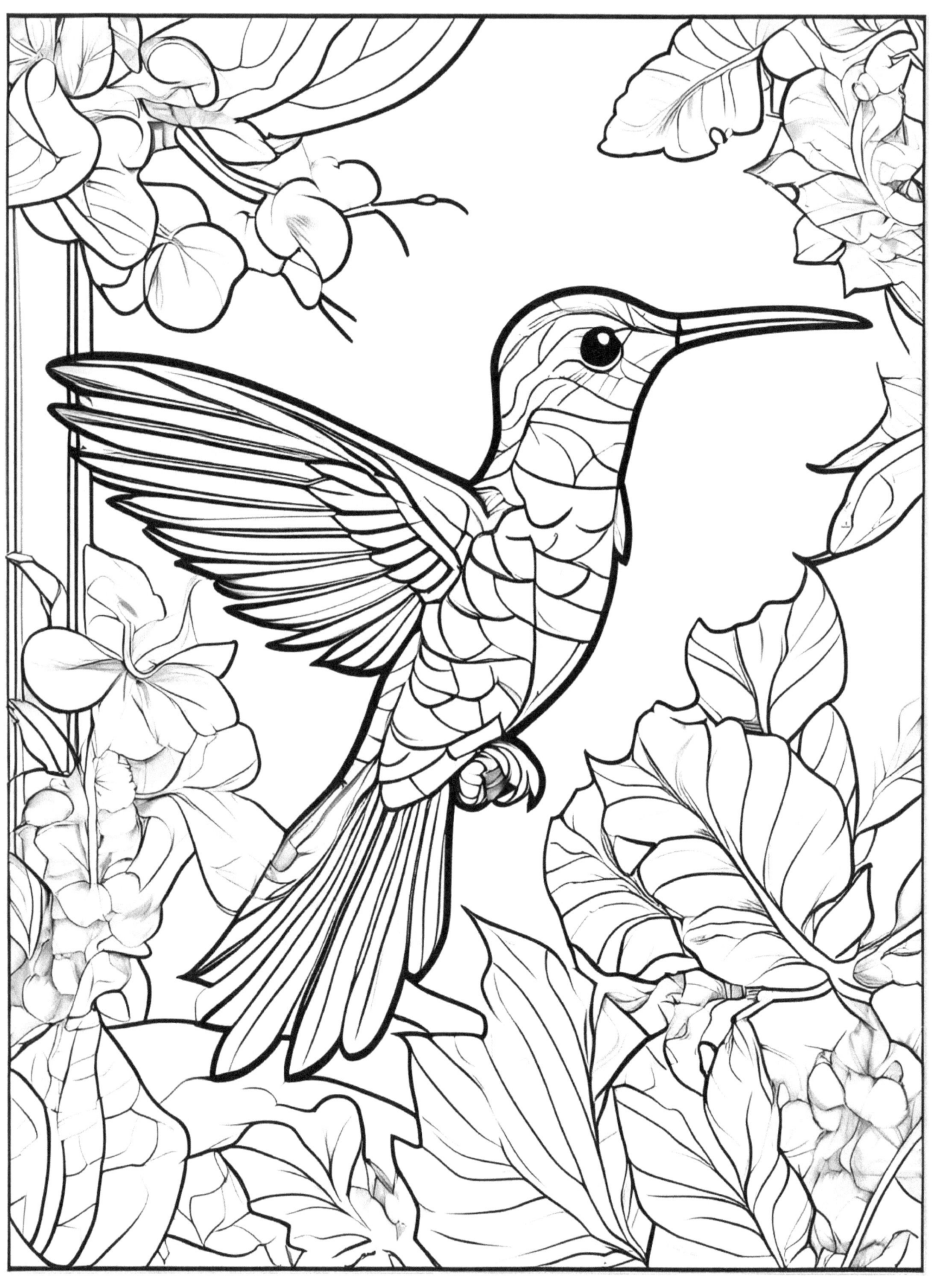

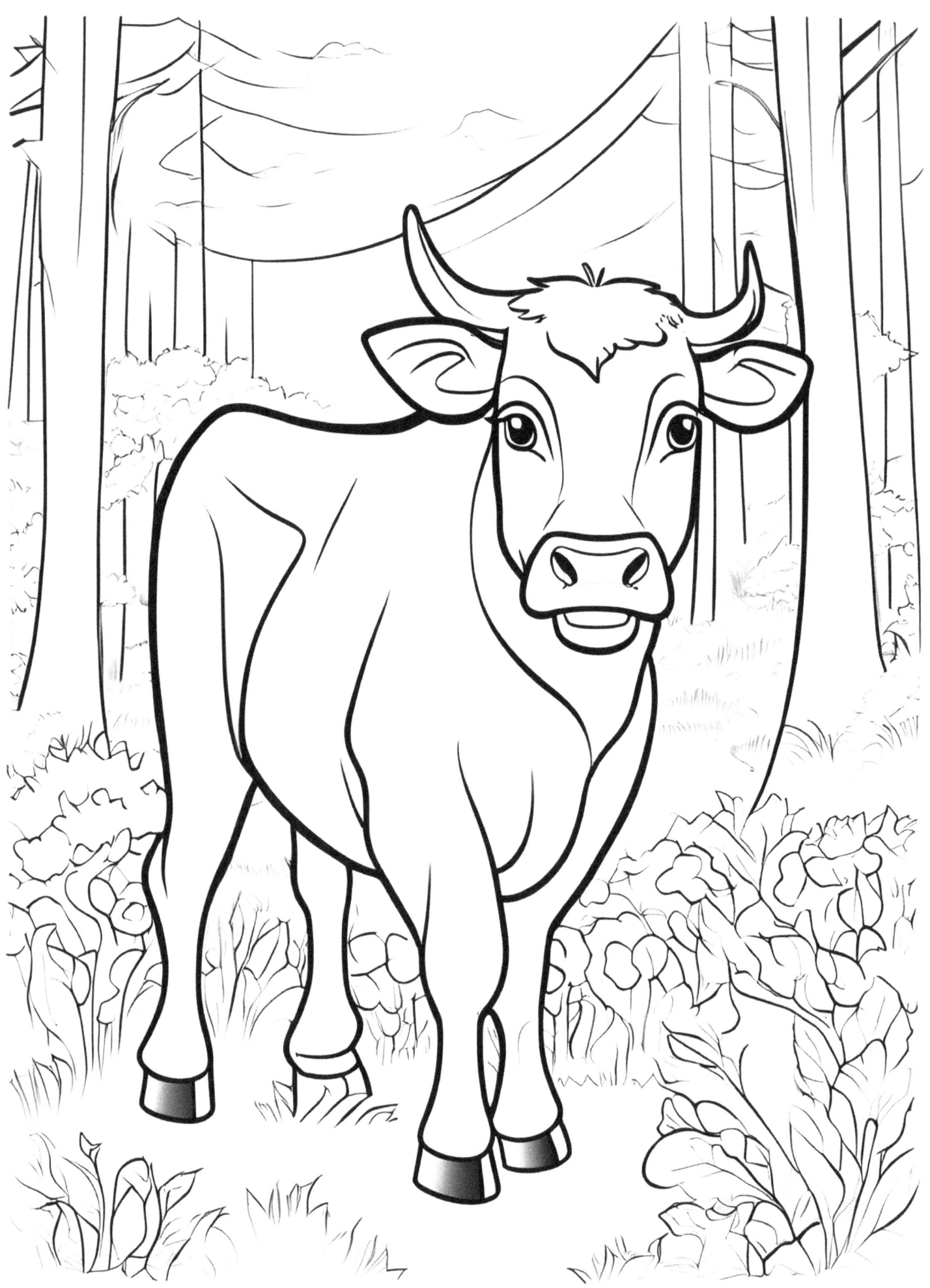

www.ingramcontent.com/pod-product-compliance
Lightning Source LLC
Chambersburg PA
CBHW062115220526
45471CB00010B/3747